United States Sailing Association

TEACHING AND COACHING

FUNDAMENTALS FOR SAILING

The national standard for quality sailing instruction

Published by the United States Sailing Association (US SAILING)
The non-profit National Governing Body for the Sport of Sailing
This is the second edition of the book originally published in 1995.

The information offered in this book reflects the cumulative experience of many volunteers involved with
sailing. It offers suggestions about how to safely teach sailing (and the operation of a "safety" boat for
supervision and rescue), but there may be other effective ways as well. It should be understood that the
application of all this information should be adapted to each "individual" situation taking into account
such factors as the age, size, experience and potential disabilities of each sailor, the type of boat being
used, the weather, location, other water activities and, all other factors which may apply. Each person
involved with sailing should accept that the sport of sailing and the conduct of any sailing or sailing
related program entail and are subject to certain inherent risks, including serious injury.

Printed in the United States of America

United States Sailing Association (US SAILING)
P. O. Box 1260, 15 Maritime Drive
Portsmouth, RI 02871 - 6015

1 - 401 - 683 - 0800 (phone)
1 - 401 - 683 - 0840 (fax)
1 - 888 - US SAIL 6 (InfoFax)
ussailing@compuserve.com (email)
www.ussailing.org (website)

ACKNOWLEDGMENTS

US SAILING would like to thank the following contributors to this manual:

Dr. Jeffrey Barsch, EdD, Professor at Ventura College in Ventura, CA, and Academic Therapy Publications in Novato, CA have contributed the Barsch Learning Style Inventory which has been adapted for use by sailing instructors.

Rich Brew, insurance executive, volunteer sailing instructor and multihull racer from Florida, has contributed the Corinthian Spirit section.

Megan Buchanan, illustrator and charter operator in the Caribbean and New England, has provided most of the current drawings for the Teaching Theory and Techniques section.

Brad Dellenbaugh, Offshore Coach at the U.S. Naval Academy, author and illustrator, has contributed the original drawings for the Teaching Theory and Techniques section.

Dr. Derrick Fries, Ph.D. in Education Administration, US SAILING Master Instructor Trainer, and Principal of the Avondale Middle School, has contributed some of the diagrams and research behind the Teaching Theory and Techniques section.

Pat Giella, teacher and US SAILING and American Red Cross instructor, has provided editorial support for the second edition.

John Kantor, Instructor and President of Longshore Sailing School, Westport, CT with more than 35 years of teaching and writing experience, has contributed the Teaching Theory and Techniques section and coordinated the development of illustrations.

Hart Kelley, Executive Director of Community Boating in Boston, has contributed material on Teaching Sailors with Learning Disabilities and Developing a Program Curriculum as well as provided extensive editing in those two sections.

Jeff Johnson, former Junior Sailing Director and current Race Administration Director at San Diego Yacht Club, has contributed the Parents in a Junior Sailing Program section.

Felix Kloman, Editor, *Risk Management Reports*, retired Principal of Towers Perrin and a Risk Management Consultant with over 35 years of worldwide consulting, writing and lecturing experience, has contributed the Risk Management section.

Timmy Larr, architect behind the Training Program, has contributed her insightful leadership to the development of these sections - always seeking to improve the materials and methods available for training instructors and students.

Ginny Long, former Training Director, has volunteered her editorial talent to the second edition.

Arn Manella, US SAILING Instructor Trainer who was formerly involved with Shake-A-Leg, has contributed material on Teaching Sailors with Physical Disabilities.

Laurie O'Brien, former Coordinator of Boating Safety for the American Camping Association, has contributed her editorial talent to some of the first edition sections.

Joni Palmer, Junior Sailing Consultant with over 20 years of experience working with junior sailors and junior sailing programs, has contributed information for the Parents in a Junior Sailing Program section.

Susie Trotman, former chair of the Training Committee, has provided editorial oversight for the second edition.

And finally, many National Faculty members have provided assistance over the years in various ways.

Sail America

This text is made possible in part by a generous grant from Sail America.

TABLE OF CONTENTS

SECTION 1 -- TEACHING THEORY AND TECHNIQUES

SECTION 2 -- CURRICULUM DEVELOPMENT

SECTION 3 -- TEACHING SAILORS WITH SPECIAL NEEDS

SECTION 4 -- RISK MANAGEMENT

SECTION 5 -- THE CORINTHIAN SPIRIT

HOW TO USE THIS MANUAL

This book is intended to help sailing instructors, coaches, judges and people involved with race management. It is laid out in sections, so you can refer to topics found in one part, with related topics found in another. **The <u>pagination</u> begins at 1 in each section** so the pages in Section 1 start as 1-1 and the pages in Section 2 start as 2-1.

Section 1 - Teaching Theory and Techniques connects the theories of learning, teaching, sports psychology, communication skills and leadership to the practice of everyday sailing instruction. Everyone processes information differently, and effective teaching is not possible without understanding this.

Section 2 - Curriculum Development offers insights on how to develop your program curriculum and strategies for dealing with parents (if you are involved with a junior sailing program). It also provides several curriculum samples.

Section 3 - Teaching Sailors with Special Needs offers insights about how to teach different people who may need special consideration and also provides insights as to how to make their sailing experience successful. These might be people with physical disabilities or people with learning disabilities.

Section 4 - Risk Management explains important Risk Management considerations.

Section 5 - The Corinthian Spirit describes the ethical behavior required of sailors and what is unique about sailing as a sport. Good sportsmanship and corinthian behavior are the cornerstones of successful sailing.

SMALL BOAT SAILING LEVEL 1 INSTRUCTOR COURSE & THIS MANUAL

The Small Boat Sailing Level 1 Instructor Course assumes that candidates are competent sailors and that they have experience in operating a safety boat. The goal is to offer insights on how to teach all kinds of people in a safe environment and to make that process fun. In addition to this manual, there are four other books that are used in the Small Boat Sailing Level 1 Instructor Course.

Small Boat Sailing Level 1 Instructor Manual covers topics from the basics to intermediate level skills and knowledge in dinghies, prams, multihulls and small daysailing keelboats. It is intended as a guide to help you fill in any gaps in your sailing knowledge. The boathandling techniques and procedures work for most sailors and sailboats.

Basic Powerboating, Safety and Rescue outlines how to use a safety boat, perform rescues of sailboats and sailors in different capsize scenarios, tow sailboats, set and retrieve marks and other race support activities.

Start Sailing Right! is the joint American Red Cross/US SAILING student text.

Boating Basics is the booklet which is approved by the National Association of State Boating Law Administrators (NASBLA). When an instructor or student completes this as part of their Small Boat Sailing Level 1 Instructor Course, they also meet any state requirements for a boating safety course.

But when you are teaching or working with sailors, ***remember that EACH SAILBOAT AND EACH SAILOR behave differently.*** **MONITOR AND ADJUST** to your particular boat and situation. Sailing and teaching sailing is not static; new and better methods are always being developed.

SECTION 1

TEACHING THEORY AND TECHNIQUES

FOREWORD

This section connects the theory of learning, teaching, sports psychology, communication skills, and leadership to the practice of everyday sailing instruction. It is intended to help the new instructor to establish fundamental skills from which to develop an individual teaching style.

New instructors should bear in mind that no text or training program can fully prepare a sailing instructor for every eventuality. So *flexibility* is the sailing instructor's watchword. The importance of maintaining that flexibility is the underlying message summed up in the Instructor Trainers' familiar catch-phrase, *monitor and adjust.*

There are few absolutes in sailing instruction. It is at least as much art as science, so plenty of room remains for an instructor's personal brand of creativity. An instructor frequently needs to be resourceful, creative, and prepared to modify and adapt any lesson plan to the circumstances of the moment.

Overall, it is good advice to remain faithful to the fundamentals without being afraid to build on them and experiment with a bit of your own. Providing for safety, fun and learning are the only unalterable requirements in sailing instruction.

HOW PEOPLE LEARN

Everybody's Different

No two students of sailing are exactly the same. Each brings a unique combination of background information, skills, hopes, fears, motives, and native talent. To some, sailing seems to come naturally; to others it is mysterious and confusing. Some easily grasp concepts but falter with hands-on skills. Others are agile and dexterous but struggle with theory and concepts. The unique mixture of attributes each student possesses presents a unique challenge to an instructor.

Left to their own devices, new untrained instructors are often inclined to teach sailing the way they learned it themselves. They reason that "if it worked for me, it will work for you too."

> ☞ **INSTRUCTORS TAKE NOTE...**
> - Different people learn differently -- including instructors.
> - Teaching methods which once helped you to learn may not be effective for all of your students.
> - If a student does not learn, the teaching is ineffective.
> - The instructor succeeds only when the student does.

Unfortunately, the "good for me/good for you" method often achieves only limited success. It appeals to the instructor's personal learning style but not necessarily to that of every student. As a result, some students learn quickly; others do not. A novice instructor, who is not familiar with the differences in the way people learn, may unfairly blame the student.

The truth is, if a student does not learn, the teaching is ineffective. All willing students have the capacity to learn. It is the instructor's job to determine how to best reach each individual and get the job done. The instructor succeeds only when the student does.

Veteran instructors can attest that a teaching technique which works well for one student may not necessarily work at all for another. If all people learned the same way, teaching sailing would be a simple matter. But people are different.

Among their personal differences is the way people perceive, store, process, and recall information. The following section explores some key elements of how people learn and how different people learn differently.

Sensory Input

Because learning is the goal of teaching, an instructor should be familiar with the learning process. Learning begins with sensory input. Sensory input is the "raw data" taken in through the five senses: seeing, hearing, smelling, tasting and feeling (touch/movement).

Information is taken in through the 5 senses.

The senses are stimulus gatherers which feed information to the brain for processing. In sailing instruction we primarily employ just three of those senses, **seeing, hearing, and feeling.**

A Selective Process. In processing, storing, and retrieving sensory information, everyone's brain operates a little differently. How we learn best and fastest varies from person to person. Some of us rely on, or favor, particular senses over others.

Specifically, some people remember best what they see. They are *visual learners*. Others remember best what they hear. They are *auditory learners*. Still others remember best what they physically feel and do. They are *kinesthetic learners*. Some people learn equally well all three ways.

All of us are capable of learning through every one of our available senses. A person who favors or relies on one sense over another is neither unable to learn, nor necessarily learns poorly, through the non-dominant senses. All senses pitch in to some degree. The proportions simply vary from one individual to another.

☞ **INSTRUCTORS TAKE NOTE...**
- When learning to sail, students use three of the five senses:
  - ✓ *Seeing*
  - ✓ *Hearing*
  - ✓ *Feeling* (physical touch, movement)
- Some students favor one sense over another -- some may learn faster by seeing or doing something rather than by just hearing it explained.

Visual Learners. A visual learner imprints and retains information most effectively when it is presented visually, such as in pictures, graphics, videos, diagrams, demonstrations, etc.

Because of this affinity for visual input, a visual learner's memory is, in a sense, photographic. For example, a visual learner may recall not just a particular illustration from a textbook, but often its location on the page as well. A visual learner would also get more out of seeing a demonstration of tacking, rigging or docking than simply hearing them explained.

Visual learners retain better and faster when they can see what they are learning.

Auditory Learners. An auditory learner learns most effectively when information is conveyed with sound. Because they remember best what they hear, auditory learners may easily recall conversations word for word. They may also recall details of each speaker's accent, tone of voice, and inflection. A person weak in auditory learning skills might only be able to remember the gist of the same conversation, while being less certain about precise phrasing and topic sequencing.

Kinesthetic Learners. A kinesthetic learner learns best by doing. Touching, physical manipulation, and the physical sensation of movement are what imprint information most easily in the kinesthetic learner's memory. A kinesthetic learner often becomes restless and bored during plain speeches and lectures, because simple listening is too passive. A kinesthetic learner retains information better when it is incorporated into some sort of physical activity.

Kinesthetic learners retain better and faster when they can touch, feel or manipulate what they are learning about.

Reading material is best conveyed to the kinesthetic by linking it to a physical activity such as underlining, highlighting, copying it over, or reciting it aloud. A favorite kinesthetic/auditory teaching technique of grade school teachers is to set repetitious rote learning to music or poetry and have the class sing or recite it together. Singing the alphabet is one familiar example.

Get Your Three Senses In. Researchers estimate that roughly 70% of all people are visual learners. About 25% are auditory learners. And approximately 5% are kinesthetic learners. Children tend to be more kinesthetic than adults.

When teaching a new sailing class, an instructor may presume there is a mix of each type of learner present. Though the instructor may not know who's who, it does not particularly matter, provided the instructor employs techniques which reach all three learning modes. If so, every student can learn. None is excluded or left behind.

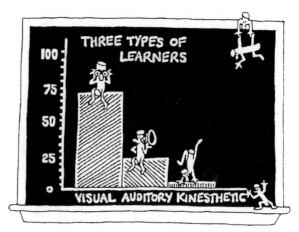

All senses help in learning, but, for many people, some senses help more than others.

Visual Teaching Techniques include the use of:

- Gestures
- Facial expressions
- Body language
- Hand signals
- Chalkboard illustrations
- Physical demonstrations

- Graphs
- Color-coding
- Text illustrations
- Handouts
- Props
- Videos

There are lots of ways to make your teaching more visual.

Auditory Teaching Techniques include the use of:

- Speech
- Whistle signals
- Loud hailers
- Audio equipment

- Instructor's voice: volume, tone, expressiveness, animation, and word choice

Auditory techniques are most helpful on the water where distance from students is greater.

Kinesthetic Teaching Techniques include the use of:

- Hands-on participation
- Land drills
- Water drills
- Reading aloud

- Rote recitation
- Copying/note taking
- Take-home projects
- Simulator practice

There are plenty of techniques to turn a boring lecture into a fun activity or game.

The simple self-test that follows will help you understand more about your own sensory preference. Try it.

SELF-TEST #1

SENSORY PREFERENCE

The following self-test is designed to help you understand whether you learn best by seeing, hearing or doing. By becoming more aware of your own learning style you will be better equipped to understand the differences in your students and adjust your teaching techniques to their needs.

This is not a timed test. You will not be graded. Simply answer each question honestly and total up your score at the end. Do not dwell on any particular question. Your first impulse usually provides the best response.

Directions: Score each of the statements below using the following point scale.

OFTEN = 5   SOMETIMES = 3   SELDOM = 1

1. _____ I remember more about a subject by listening than reading about it.

2. _____ I am better at following written directions than oral ones.

3. _____ When learning something new I like to jot down notes to review later.

4. _____ I bear down hard when I write with a pen or pencil.

5. _____ I require explanations of graphs, diagrams or visual directions.

6. _____ I like working with tools.

7. _____ I like and have little difficulty developing graphs and charts.

8. _____ I can easily tell if sounds match when I hear pairs of sounds.

9. _____ I remember things best when I write them down several times.

10. _____ I can understand and follow directions on maps.

11. _____ I learn school material better by listening to lectures and recordings.

12. _____ I play with coins, keys or other objects in my pockets.

13. _____ I can remember how to spell words better if I say the letters out loud rather than write them down.

14. _____ I understand news items better when I read them in the paper rather than listening to the radio.

15. _____ I chew gum or snack while I study.

16. _____ I find that the best way to remember something is to visualize it in my mind.

17. _____ I learn to spell words by writing imaginary letters with my finger tips.

18. _____ I prefer to listen to a good lecture or speech than read a text on the same subject.

19. _____ I am good at working and solving jigsaw puzzles and mazes.

20. _____ I grip or fiddle with objects while I am learning something new.

21. _____ I'd rather listen to the news on a radio than read about it in a newspaper.

22. _____ I get information on interesting subjects by reading about them.

23. _____ I am uncomfortable hugging, handshaking, touching others, etc.

24. _____ I am better at following spoken directions than written ones.

Scoring: Copy the point value from each of the above questions onto the correspondingly numbered spaces below. Total each column to obtain your personal sensory preference values.

VISUAL		AUDITORY		KINESTHETIC	
No.	Pts.	No.	Pts.	No.	Pts.
2	___	1	___	4	___
3	___	5	___	6	___
7	___	8	___	9	___
10	___	11	___	12	___
14	___	13	___	15	___
16	___	18	___	17	___
20	___	21	___	19	___
22	___	24	___	23	___
Total = ___		Total = ___		Total = ___	

Adapted from the original Barsch Learning Style Inventory by Dr. Jeffrey Barsch, EdD. with permission of Academic Therapy Publications, 20 Commercial Blvd., Novato, CA 94947

Multiple Pathways Teaching. As a rule, the more student sensory pathways an instructor can bring into play the better. A student's retention is generally higher and there is less confusion when multiple sensory pathways receive an integrated unambiguous message simultaneously.

Ideally, the student should see, hear, and do, all at once. Auditory teaching techniques, such as lecturing, may work adequately for highly auditory learners. Visual techniques, such as demonstrations, may work fine for highly visual learners. Yet, combining auditory with visual teaching techniques (e.g., explaining while demonstrating) works even better for both auditory *and* visual learners. Better still, blending visual, auditory *and* kinesthetic techniques (e.g., telling and showing while the students are doing) improves learning for all students.

Multiple Pathways Teaching -
using 3 senses instead of just 1.

The use of integrated visual, auditory, and kinesthetic teaching techniques allows every student to learn the way that suits him or her best, while receiving the same reinforcing message through their non-dominant senses. Learning takes place better and faster, and a class of students is more likely to progress at a uniform pace. As a bonus, multiple pathway teaching livens up the teaching environment, makes it more fun, and helps to raise motivation and morale.

> ☞ INSTRUCTORS TAKE
>   NOTE...
> To reach all types of learners:
>   ✓ *Show them* (visual)
>   ✓ *Tell them* (auditory)
>   ✓ *Let them do it*
>   (kinesthetic)

Left Brain/Right Brain

Sensory input is only the "raw data" of learning. It needs further processing to become useful. The brain processes sensory input by neurochemically sorting and transforming it into what we call awareness, thought and understanding. The manner in which our brain perceives and responds to the surrounding environment is sometimes characterized by psychologists as being either *right-brained* or *left-brained*.

The human brain has two distinct *cerebral hemispheres*, right and left. Each side specializes in particular mental activities. Similar to being right or left-handed, some people's brains tend to rely on one hemisphere more than the other when processing information. Because each hemisphere specializes in different mental activities, its relative contribution often gives rise to distinctive thought patterns and learning traits in different individuals.

Some of the principal characteristics and mental activities associated with each hemisphere are listed below:

Left Brain	Right Brain
• Abstract thinking	• Concrete thinking
• Analytic thinking	• Intuitive thinking
• Auditory activity	• Visual activity
• Deductive reasoning	• Inductive reasoning
• Logical thinking	• Holistic thinking

Though a bit technical, the above offers further insight into why people sometimes think, learn, and communicate so differently. It applies to instructors as much as students, so it suggests why some students and instructors seem to see eye to eye, while others appear to operate on very different wavelengths, mutually confused and frustrated.

To find out more about your own brain hemisphere preference take the self-test on the following page.

Artists and Engineers. While some people may rely on one brain hemisphere more than the other, we all still use all parts of our brain. It is simply a matter of proportion. Everybody is a bit different. The blend of proportions form a recipe, of sorts, for our individual thought patterns.

Not everyone thinks alike.

SELF-TEST #2

HEMISPHERIC PREFERENCE

Directions: Circle the number corresponding to the answer which describes you best.

1. In school I was/am usually better at:
    1. math
    2. art
2. In school I was/am usually better at:
    1. languages
    2. crafts
3. I normally reach decisions by:
    1. step by step analysis
    2. getting a "feel" for the solution as a whole
4. In work or personal life I usually follow hunches only when I can justify them logically.
    1. True
    2. False
5. I often follow hunches which "feel" right even though they may not seem logical.
    1. True
    2. False
6. Have you ever had the feeling, before being told, that a very close friend or immediate family member was sick or in serious trouble?
    1. Yes
    2. No
7. In sketching maps, pictures or plans I have a better than average sense of direction and how the elements relate to one another.
    1. True
    2. False
8. It is more gratifying to me when a personal project:
    1. is well planned
    2. contributes to something new
9. I find problem solving more satisfying when I:
    1. think it all through carefully
    2. try fitting interesting new ideas together
10. Frequently I have hunches about upcoming events which prove to be correct?
    1. True
    2. False

Score: Add the numbers you have circled.

        10 - 14 = left brain   16 - 20 = right brain   15 = whole brain, no dominance

A COMPARISON OF LEFT-MODE AND RIGHT-MODE CHARACTERISTICS

Left-Mode

Verbal: Using words to name, describe or define.

Analytic: Figuring things out step-by-step and part-by-part.

Symbolic: Using a symbol to stand for something. For example, the + sign stands for the process of addition.

Abstract: Taking out a small bit of information and using it to represent the whole thing.

Temporal: Keeping track of time, sequencing one thing after another. Doing first things first, second things second, etc.

Rational: Drawing conclusions based on reason and fact.

Digital: Using numbers as in counting.

Logical: Drawing conclusions based on logic. One thing following another in logical order. For example, a mathematical theorem or well stated argument.

Linear: Thinking in terms of linked ideas, one thought directly following another, often leading to a convergent conclusion.

Right-Mode

Non-Verbal: Awareness of things, but minimal connection with words.

Synthetic: Putting things together to form wholes.

Concrete: Relating to things as they are, at the present moment.

Analogical: Seeing likeness between things.

Non-Temporal: Without a sense of time.

Non-Rational: Not requiring a basis of reason or facts; willingness to suspend judgment.

Spatial: Seeing where things are in relation to other things, and how parts go together to form a whole.

Intuitive: Making leaps of insight, often based on incomplete patterns, hunches, feelings, or visual images.

Holistic: Seeing whole things all at once; perceiving the overall patterns and structures, often leading to divergent conclusions.

What Am I??? New instructors ought to spend some time becoming familiar with their own learning and problem solving characteristics. An instructor's personal learning style favoritism or bias could blind him to the learning needs of students who require a different approach.

The previous self-tests should help you to understand a bit more about your own learning style. After taking the self-tests ask yourself:

1. Do I favor one sensory pathway over another?

2. Do I respond better to one teaching technique than another?

3. How much does it influence the way I teach and communicate with others.

4. Do I recognize and understand those differences in others?

5. Am I patient with those who learn differently?

6. What modifications could I make in my teaching style to accommodate them?

☞ **INSTRUCTORS TAKE NOTE...**
- Understanding your own learning style is the best starting point before teaching others. It includes understanding how you yourself perceive, process and store information.
- The Sensory Preference Self-Test will help you understand your own strengths and weaknesses in how you perceive the world around you.
- The Hemispheric Preference Self-Test will help you understand more about how you personally process information, solve problems and respond to your environment.

Monitor and Adjust. You should be prepared to adjust your teaching style to reach all your students, not just a few. To do that well it is helpful to know yourself, understand your students, carefully monitor student responsiveness, and adjust your teaching style to meet them on their own mental turf.

PSYCHOLOGY OF LEARNING

Behavioral Psychology offers a good deal of insight into individual learning behavior in sailing instruction. In experimental psychology, the training process is called *conditioning*.

Conditioning

Conditioned Response. Behaviorists hold that the *conditioned response* explains why we do what we do. They say that behavior is learned, shaped, repeated, or curbed by a variety of rewards and punishments in our environment. Put succinctly, people tend to do what is pleasant or rewarding, and tend not to do what is unpleasant or results in punishment. Accordingly, a system of rewards, no rewards, or punishment can be used to bring about, modify, or discourage specific behavior patterns.

Positive Reinforcement. In the *conditioned response* a desired behavior is encouraged by the instructor by pairing it with a reward called *positive reinforcement*. To *condition* equipment care, for example, every time a student cleans and stores the equipment properly the instructor would respond with positive reinforcement. Positive reinforcement is something desirable or rewarding, such as praise: "You did a very careful and thorough job with the equipment clean-up today, Tammy. Well done. I'm very pleased."

> ☞ **INSTRUCTORS TAKE NOTE...**
> - Positive reinforcement is encouraging and stimulates behavior.
> - If a behavior is not positively reinforced, it will extinguish.

The idea is to pair the desired behavior with the "reward" of a compliment. The reward is conditional. It depends on the subject's display of the correct behavior, hence the name *conditioned* response. The underlying intent, of course, is to encourage Tammy to get in the everyday habit of keeping the equipment clean, neat and orderly. Such regular positive reinforcement encourages regular positive behavior. Positive reinforcement is the corner-stone of motivation, morale and performance.

Positive Reinforcement - there's nothing like a pat on the back.

Extinction

A specific behavior is less likely to occur if it is no longer positively reinforced. Eventually it may cease altogether. In psychology that process is called *extinction.*

If, for example, the instructor never again seems to notice or care about Tammy's hard work in making things shipshape, she may eventually stop putting so much effort into it. Once she no longer perceives any further benefit, she may no longer bother to do it at all. At that point the behavior extinguishes.

Extinction -
don't overlook a job well-done or it may not happen again.

Students depend on their instructor to teach them the correct way to perform a task and to convey the need and value of it. An instructor's failure to acknowledge or positively reinforce a student's effort may be perceived by the student as indifference. Indifference, whether real or imagined, on the part of the instructor naturally leads to non-performance on the part of the student; because it implies the task is not very important.

The conditioning process is like a series of small unwritten agreements between instructor and student. "I'll do this if you do that." The student's expectation of repeat reward encourages repeat behavior. If suddenly the reward no longer comes, it signals to the student that the deal is off. The *conditioned behavior* then begins to extinguish. So, to encourage or maintain a student's important behavior patterns an instructor should keep up his/her end of the bargain. *Positively reinforce desirable behavior or risk its extinction.*

Intermittent Reinforcement

After a period of steady conditioning, where reward is *always* given for a desired behavior, sometimes intermittent positive reinforcement may be substituted without risking extinction. For example, in time Tammy may become so accustomed to tidying up the equipment that eventually only occasional praise may be required to inspire her to keep up her good work.

Switching from a regular (every time) to an intermittent (occasional) positive reinforcement schedule may even become necessary after awhile. After a certain amount of conditioning, positive reinforcement can go stale and lose its appeal. In other words, too much of a good thing is no longer as good.

Tammy could become so accustomed to her daily compliments, for example, that she may begin taking them for granted. As a result, the quality or consistency of her work may start to slip. In such a case it would be better for the instructor to ease up and provide only occasional reinforcement, praising Tammy only when her work is truly exceptional rather than simply good. Switching to an intermittent reinforcement schedule at the right time raises the stakes, restores the perceived value of the positive reinforcement, and leads to improved performance. Intermittent reinforcement is the motivational basis for coaching students and athletes to higher performance.

Self-Reinforcement

In time, certain behavior can become self-reinforcing. An internal motivation develops so the behavior no longer requires outside positive reinforcement. Tammy, for instance, may eventually learn to take independent personal pride in the quality of her work. She may feel good about herself and the neat appearance of her equipment, so she wants to keep it tidy even when no one else is likely to notice. At that point Tammy has developed her own internal positive reinforcement which no longer depends on the instructor's praise. This is an important goal of the instructor's efforts, generating students' self-motivation.

Behavior Modification

For the most part, people are inclined to do what is fun, pleasant or rewarding. Naturally they avoid what is uncomfortable or unpleasant. It's really just common sense.

Though an instructor may use plenty of positive reinforcement to encourage good sailing habits, there are also some negative influences which may be employed to shape, encourage or eliminate certain behaviors. They usually come into play more often when teaching children than adults. They include:

1. **Withholding a positive reinforcer**
   Example: "We will not break for ice cream until everything is shipshape."
2. **Removing a negative stimulus**
   Example: "You don't have to do your shore chores today if all the boats are shipshape within 5 minutes."
3. **Applying a negative stimulus (punishment)**
   Example: "You have repeatedly neglected your boat, so today you have to clean all the boats yourself."

Harmful or dangerous excesses in a student's behavior which must be stopped immediately may need to be controlled with instant punishment. For example, if Dale teasingly shoves Tammy off the dock, the instructor may issue Dale an immediate stern reprimand to put a quick end to his horseplay.

Avoidance Behavior

A shortcoming of punishment, however, is that it sometimes oversteps its bounds and represses or extinguishes an entire range of otherwise desirable behavior.

A student who has an unpleasant (punishing) experience, such as a capsize, a collision or a crash landing, may later refuse to take the helm again or, worse, give up sailing altogether. Though the only mistake may have been a single momentary steering error, a student may overreact to the past embarrassment by avoiding the entire situation. The student may simply refuse to steer again.

Sailing is a recreational activity. It should be fun. A student's avoidance behavior is a signal to the instructor that the fun is missing and needs to be salvaged. Avoidance behavior is usually the product of fear. So the source of the fear must be identified and addressed.

Fear

Fear can be a serious impediment to learning. It may sometimes go unnoticed and unchecked, because it is often hidden behind avoidance behavior. A student's fear of something, such as heeling, high-wind jibes or docking, can dominate the student's thinking to the exclusion of all else. Because the frightened mind tends to focus on avoiding the fear-producing situation, both memory and reason may be suspended until the fear passes. The distracting influence of fear can make effective teaching and learning extremely difficult.

Reluctant students who are impassive, who avoid involvement, or who regularly defer certain tasks to others, may actually be avoiding the activity out of fear. It may be a fear of failure, fear of embarrassment, or even fear of some imagined danger. Just as a child with a burned finger gives fire a wide berth, a sailing student may be reluctant to approach a fear or anxiety producing situation on a sailboat.

> ☞ **INSTRUCTORS TAKE NOTE...**
> - Any unpleasantness can be punishing, e.g., extreme temperatures, uncomfortable clothing, an overcrowded cockpit, an uncooperative crewmate, an embarrassing error, a collision, etc.
> - Negative experiences can lead to fear, and fear can lead to avoidance behavior.
> - A student who develops a sudden headache or complains of nausea may be expressing hidden fear.
> - Fear takes the fun out of sailing. When it is no longer fun, the student will eventually stop sailing altogether.

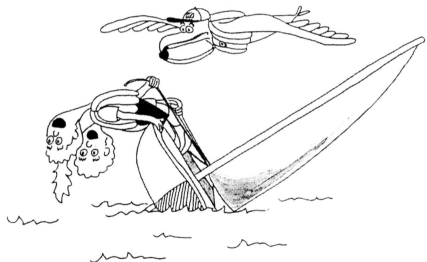

Don't let fear replace learning.

Instructors need to recognize fear and compensate for it by restoring positive reinforcement to the fearful situation. It requires patience and understanding. Often, working through a trouble-some maneuver side by side with a student, offering encouragement, bolstering self-esteem, and creating a positively reinforcing series of personal successes, will help to allay fear, restore confidence, and rebuild positive motivation.

Motivation

Learning comes much more quickly when a student is comfortable, relaxed, and willing. A student is not simply a passive receptacle for information but an active participant in a learning process. It is a partnership between instructor and student. As in any partnership, willing and earnest teamwork can make all the difference. Willingness stems from motivation, and motivation may stem from a variety of sources.

There are three categories of principal motivating factors:

1. Extrinsic rewards
2. Intrinsic rewards
3. Negative sanctions

Extrinsic Rewards. Extrinsic rewards include all of the positive reinforcement which comes from others. They include:

- **Tangible** keepsakes and mementos such as trophies, plaques, diplomas, certificates, prizes, T-shirts, etc.

- **Intangibles** such as approval, praise, compliments, encouragement, admiration, enthusiasm, friendship, or respect of instructors, parents or peers.

Extrinsic rewards are particularly helpful tools when teaching beginners, because beginners need a good deal of initial encouragement. In everyday teaching and coaching, instructor praise and encouragement are the most effective and economical extrinsic awards.

> ☞ **INSTRUCTORS TAKE NOTE...**
> - Don't keep awards a secret. Let your students know about them in advance, so they will have something to strive for.
> - Awards motivate best when presented publicly. Peer approval motivates better than keepsakes.
> - Award ceremonies motivate best when they are brief and well focused.
> - "Praise in public, reprimand in private."

Tangible awards are most effective as a motivator when they are announced *before* instruction begins, rather than after. They should not be kept a secret. The students' hope of winning a prize or getting an award can silently boost their motivation and effort every day.

Extrinsic rewards have a more far-reaching effect when every student stands a realistic chance of winning. If they are few and too exclusive, they have limited appeal as a general motivator. While high achievers certainly deserve their due honors, the runners-up could also benefit from some recognition and formal encouragement. Simple awards or citations, such as "Most Improved," "Shipshape," or "Perfect Attendance" can be very meaningful, appealing, and effective in raising the broader group morale.

There is an old saying, "**praise in public; reprimand in private**." Praising worthy achievement in public leverages its reinforcing effect dramatically, particularly when praise is given in the presence of those whom the recipient respects. Taking the time to honor or appreciate a deserving individual with public recognition, praise, or thanks, pays motivation dividends for a long time. Both the recipient and all those present at the ceremony may be inspired by it. Newspaper or newsletter publicity can further stretch the benefit of the positive reinforcement.

Extrinsic Rewards

Reprimands in public, on the other hand, often have just the opposite effect and should be avoided. The unpredictably damaging effect of a public reprimand on a student's overall morale and motivation should not be underestimated. "Reprimand in private" is wise advice which is all too often overlooked. If disciplining unruly students becomes necessary, it is often best done in private where fragile egos can be protected from public view. It is only the behavior, not a student's self-esteem, which should be challenged. When skillfully and discreetly handled, a private reprimand can be transformed into a constructive positive reinforcer instead of a damaging and demoralizing incident.

Intrinsic Rewards. Intrinsic rewards are intangible self-reinforcing influences which develop from the emotions of the individual student. They may be the pride of accomplishment, the sense of triumph in achieving excellence or mastering a difficult challenge. They also include feelings of enhanced self-worth, satisfaction in overcoming a fear, the thrill of participation, enjoying the company of friends, or simple fun and excitement. Intrinsic rewards are self-reinforcing and form the basis of positive long-term self-motivation.

Intrinsic Rewards

The Criticism Sandwich

When teaching a new skill, an instructor's casual blunt criticism may sometimes discourage the very behavior it is intended to improve. Critical remarks should be constructive and worded tactfully. When an instructor critiques a student's performance, negative feedback should be surrounded with encouragement. If, for example, Tammy oversteers when tacking, and the instructor simply comments, "That was a lousy tack," Tammy learns nothing useful and may very well feel hurt or discouraged by her instructor's terse and callous remark.

In a *criticism sandwich* the instructor gets the message across without the sting by layering negative feedback, like a sandwich, in between slices of positive feedback.

1. The instructor starts off with a positive remark, such as "Good effort, Tammy. You nearly nailed it that time."
2. Then the instructor slips in the negative part of the feedback, "but you oversteered a bit," tactfully sparing Tammy's ego by focusing on the specific part of the maneuver which did not measure up.
3. Then the instructor constructively offers a remedy to the problem, "begin straightening your course a little sooner after the tack." And finally the instructor leaves the student with a positive and encouraging comment, "Let me see you try it again. I know you can do this."

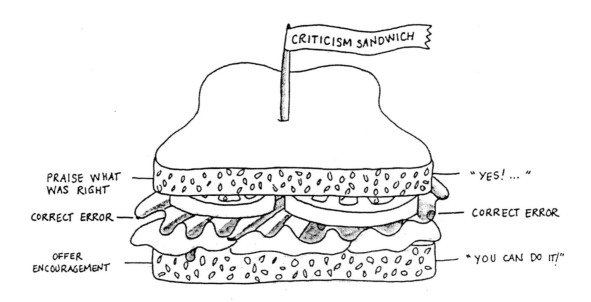

A tactful *criticism sandwich* is perceived positively and can boost motivation. Instructors need to be aware of how their comments are perceived and felt, so they can avoid the pitfalls of negativity. Obvious and potentially embarrassing student mistakes, such as accidental collisions, do not need to be pointed out at all. Announcing the event across the water to the whole group may only add humiliation to an already embarrassing situation. It would be more constructive to use the experience as a teaching tool, helping the students understand what went wrong and how to prevent a recurrence.

```
☞ INSTRUCTORS
    TAKE NOTE...
Remember what it feels like to learn
a new skill and respect the integrity
of your students as they go through
this learning process.
```

Positive remarks, praise and encouragement bring out the best in students. Negative remarks often bring out the worst. A student's eager willingness to learn should be carefully cultivated and never jeopardized by an instructor's insensitive or careless remarks. Although sailing is just a recreational pastime, teaching it is sometimes a very personal and delicate matter. It can either encourage or discourage a student's further pursuit of the sport. It is a responsibility which conscientious instructors should not take lightly.

COMMUNICATION

Productive teaching begins with clear communication. Communication is successful when an intended message is accurately conveyed by the instructor and understood by the student. But it is not a simple matter of, "I talk. You listen." The everyday communication between instructor and student has many elements. Some are obvious, others quite subtle. The following section explores the complexities of communicating effectively, both on and off the water.

☞ **INSTRUCTORS TAKE NOTE...**
It is important to continually *monitor* that your sailing students understand what you are trying to teach.

Format

Group Instruction. In group instruction the students usually learn a good deal from each other by observing each other's boat and sail handling. Frequently students compare experiences, share ideas and informally tutor each other during and after class. They meet new people and develop friendships. They often encourage and support one another through the trust which evolves naturally from teamwork. Additionally, group instruction is generally more cost and time effective, since the student/instructor ratio is higher.

The main disadvantage of group instruction is less individual attention. An instructor cannot possibly personally attend to everyone at once.

It is important for instructors to bear in mind that even when sailing students are taught in groups, each individual still requires a certain degree of personal custom care. The prudent instructor is always conscious of the fact that a class is composed of individuals. So individual feedback and personal encouragement is far more useful to a student than a sweeping, "good job, everyone". Because people learn differently and at different paces, varying amounts of personal attention may be necessary and should be expected. Nevertheless, personal attention should be allocated judiciously to avoid the appearance of playing favorites or neglecting the needs of the larger group.

Private Lessons. Private one-on-one instruction differs considerably from group instruction. Each has advantages and disadvantages.

In private lessons the instructor is free to concentrate exclusively on one student. Both the lesson plan and its pace can be custom tailored to the individual. For some students, particularly those with time constraints or special learning needs, private lessons are the ideal way to learn to sail.

Disadvantages to private lessons are the absence of other sailboats for visual comparison, and the missing positive social element of shared recreation.

In a private lesson the relationship between instructor and student is analogous to that of doctor and patient. A doctor examines a patient, makes a diagnosis, prescribes a course of treatment, then monitors and adjusts the therapy as the patient responds. Similarly, an instructor assesses a student's ability, maturity, and learning style, makes a diagnosis as to what deficiencies need attention, prescribes and administers an appropriate lesson plan, then monitors and adjusts the dosage depending on response.

Distractions

Anything competing for the student's attention is a distraction. Distractions draw attention away from the specific lesson and interfere with learning. Because of distractions a conveyed message may come through fragmented, distorted or not at all.

Distractions may come from the surrounding environment, student preoccupations, or even the instructor's own appearance and behavior. To assist student concentration an instructor should seek and eliminate as many distractions as possible. Distractions in sailing instruction may be divided into three categories: environmental, student, and instructor.

> ☞ **INSTRUCTORS TAKE NOTE...**
> An instructor should arrive early and prearrange the teaching environment as much as practical to minimize distractions and help focus student concentration. As the saying goes, "*If it's not part of the solution, it's part of the problem.*"

Environmental Distractions include noises, sights, odors, extreme temperatures, uncomfortable or badly arranged seating, poor lighting, poor ventilation, other students, intervening boating traffic, and anything else in or around the teaching environment which might capture the student's attention at the expense of the lesson plan.

Be sure the teaching area is free of as many environmental distractions as possible.

Student Distractions include personal discomforts or preoccupations such as fatigue, illness, pain, hunger, thirst, family problems, uncomfortable clothing, fear or nervousness, a vision or hearing impairment, emotional or physical maladies, and any other personal or private matters which may weigh on a student's mind and compete for attention.

Instructor Distractions include peculiar mannerisms, gestures, or speech patterns, poor hygiene or grooming, inappropriate dress or language, poor attitude, bad manners, or any other attributes which may unnecessarily draw attention away from the intended message.

> ☞ **INSTRUCTORS TAKE NOTE...**
> Provide bathroom and refreshment breaks at appropriate intervals (generally 60 to 90 minutes). They cost a little time, but they make structured time much more productive,

> ☞ **INSTRUCTORS TAKE NOTE...**
> Look in a mirror before class. See what you look like. Prepare your lesson plan well so you can be relaxed with the material. Have someone videotape you teaching a class, so you can see for yourself how you appear.

Classroom Presentation Skills

Preparation. Preparation for teaching should begin long before it starts. In a format with no pre-designed curriculum or course outline, a detailed written plan should be prepared daily by the instructor. It should have clearly stated goals, topic sequence, teaching method, equipment requirements, time allotments, and a method for evaluating results.

Before class all teaching materials, handouts, audio and visual aids and props should be checked carefully. Once class begins, it should flow smoothly and without interruption. Awkward pauses to locate, organize, or repair teaching aids shatter student concentration, diminish confidence, and make it difficult to maintain control of the teaching environment.

Repetition is a normal and necessary part of teaching. The more important the point, the more important it is to repeat it. There are several good reasons to repeat yourself. Some students may not have been paying attention the first time. Some may have not heard you clearly. Some may have not understood fully. Repetition gives them another chance to learn and you another chance to succeed. There is an old saying, 'three times for the average mind.'

Multiple Pathways Teaching. Untrained or careless instructors sometimes refer to classroom teaching sessions as *lectures*. The word *lecture* carries a negative connotation and should be avoided. Lectures and speeches are very boring to many students, particularly to the visual and kinesthetic learners. Unless the instructor is a truly gifted or charismatic speaker, plain lecturing is a poor teaching technique. It appeals mainly to the auditory learners present, only 25% of a typical group. A trained instructor uses many communication techniques in classroom teaching besides simple speech.

Some instructors prefer to call classroom teaching *chalk talks*, because they illustrate their point on a chalkboard while they speak. Students retain more from chalk talks than from plain lectures because of the visual assistance of the chalkboard. Visual aids, of course, appeal to the visual learners; and both auditory and visual learners learn better when they see and hear the same message together. Chalk talks appeal to a much broader audience than plain lectures, roughly 95% vs. 25%.

Better still, combining auditory, visual, and kinesthetic teaching techniques usually achieves the best results of all. Neither auditory nor visual techniques appeal to the kinesthetic learner as much as *doing*. Kinesthetic learners often fidget and lose concentration in a sedentary or passive learning environment. Veteran instructors know that active physical involvement coordinated with auditory and visual support works best for virtually every type of learner.

An instructor who simply stands still and lectures on how to furl a sail will get very poor learning results. An instructor who demonstrates, using an actual sail, while explaining furling will have far greater success. But the instructor who takes it a step further, getting the students physically involved, hands-on, manipulating a real sail will achieve the best results of all.

> Seeing,
> hearing and
> doing --

these three methods combined teach the best

> ☞ **INSTRUCTORS TAKE NOTE...**
> *Chalk talks* should be kept to 10 minutes because of a student's attention span and comprehension ability for new material.

Illustrate your point whenever possible. Diagrams and hands-on demonstrations are what hold the attention of the visual and kinesthetic learners.

> ☞ **INSTRUCTORS TAKE NOTE...**
> Passive "sit and listen" lectures are not very effective for most types of learners. Chalk talks get much better results, because they include a **visual** component. Better still are interactive **(kinesthetic)** teaching techniques which also involve active student participation.

Illustrate Your Point. Get in the habit of drawing diagrams, writing outlines, or somehow illustrating your key points on a chalkboard, where they can visually reinforce your lesson and silently repeat it as often as your students glance at the board. Strategically pausing now and then to draw on a chalkboard also provides students with some helpful assimilation time and you with a moment to collect your thoughts.

When giving chalk talks, avoid talking into the board. Pause to write or draw as needed; but then stand aside and turn to face your students when you speak. Block no one's view, and be sure everyone can hear you clearly. Be conscious of the visual cut-off angle your body creates. When giving chalk talks, demonstrations or any presentation, arrange student seating in a semi-circle or horseshoe large enough for everyone to see clearly.

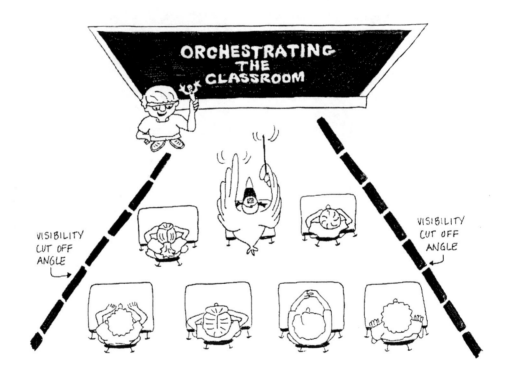

Stand aside so everyone can see.

Utilizing Resources. There are many books, magazines, videos and teaching aids which can be used to augment your teaching. Some, like the *Small Boat Sailor Certification Record Book* (known as the "Little Red Book"), and the *Start Sailing Right!* book and video tapes, are available from US SAILING along with many other products. Don't forget your local libraries, museums, marine stores, book stores, sailing lofts, boat builders, sailing related industries and "hot shot" sailors --all are excellent resources.

Interactive Teaching

Not every topic, however, lends itself easily to hands-on kinesthetic teaching techniques. Some topics involve concepts, rather than physical skills, and are the most challenging when teaching kinesthetic learners. Interactive teaching is quite often an effective method. The following are among the most common interactive teaching techniques in sailing instruction.

The Discovery Method is also known as the *Socratic Method*. It involves posing a series of easily answered questions which guide the class to a conclusion foreseen by the instructor. In response to the instructor's "loaded" questions the students volunteer answers. Each answer is a step toward a broader conclusion. This method works particularly well if the pace is quick and lively, the instructor illustrates each point on the chalkboard and the instructor actively involves and draws out responses from every student.

> ☞ **INSTRUCTORS TAKE NOTE...**
> Classroom teaching techniques include:
> *Non-Interactive*
> 1. Lecture (auditory)
> 2. Chalk talk (auditory and visual)
> 3. Video
> *Interactive*
> 1. Discovery Method
> 2. Challenge Technique
> 3. Listing Technique
> 4. Pros and Cons Technique
> 5. Student presentations

Example:
Question 1: "What stops a sailboat from sideslipping?"
Answer   1: "Centerboard, daggerboard or keel"

Question 2: "On which point of sail is it needed least?"
Answer   2: "Running"

Question 3: "How can you reduce underwater resistance on a centerboard boat when running?"
Answer   3: "Raise the centerboard"

The Discovery Method helps a student assimilate information by pressing the student to focus on the topic, think independently and actively respond. It also provides the instructor with valuable feedback on each student's level of understanding.

Socrates taught by asking leading questions.

Teaching by guided discovery does not always draw out the desired responses right away. Sometimes the question must be repeated or rephrased. Reaching a desired conclusion sometimes can be unpredictably time consuming, so it may not always be a practical teaching technique when class time runs short.

When that is the case, a discovery/chalk-talk combination can help speed the lesson along. To save time, the instructor retreats to the speedier, self-pacing chalk-talk method of presenting the material, pausing only as time allows to challenge students with leading questions. By limiting interaction this way, the instructor gains more control over the pace. The trade-off is the risk of sacrificing some effectiveness. Maintaining as much active student participation as time and circumstances allow is the key to overall effectiveness in classroom teaching techniques.

The Challenge Technique is a slight variation on the Discovery Method. In the Challenge Technique the instructor also asks leading questions but calls on students at random without seeking volunteers.

> Example: "Susie, Which way should you move the tiller to jibe?"

In a shy, passive or reluctant group it presses every student to engage the topic and actively participate in the discussion. The class is likely to remain particularly alert, since no student knows who may be called on next for a response.

The Challenge Technique has the potential to be misused as a way to "catch" someone who was not paying attention. Calling on students by saying their names first, then asking a question, will draw their attention and avoid embarrassing those who may have been momentarily distracted.

The Listing Technique is another variation on the Discovery Method. It is most suitable for teaching topics with a series of related elements.

> Example: "What items do you think ought to be included on a pre-sail checklist."

Each student is invited to provide an answer. The instructor lists the responses on the chalkboard. As the list grows, it serves as a constant visual reinforcer, imprinting the information in the students' visual memory. The technique helps maintain the class' attention, because the students are active contributors to a visible product.

The Pros and Cons Technique is a further variation on the Listing Technique. It is useful for topics where the intent is to emphasize or clarify advantages, disadvantages, differences and limitations.

> Example: "Compared to planing hull vessels, can you think of any performance advantages or disadvantages of displacement hulls?"

The instructor makes two side-by-side lists of student responses on the board, one for advantages, one for disadvantages. The two lists visually reinforce the students' auditory input. The side-by-side display encourages visual comparison, and the interaction helps keep kinesthetic learners engaged.

Verbal Communication

This refers to what you say and how you sound when you say it. There are several key elements:

Voice quality. Some voices are easy to listen to; others can be quite dull. The quality of an instructor's voice can help or hinder the learning process. Be conscious of the sound of your voice. Do you enunciate clearly so everyone can understand every word? Do you use an appropriate volume, projecting your voice so you can be heard clearly in the back of the room? Does the pitch and tone of your voice vary with enthusiasm and emphasis, or does it remain flat and monotonous?

Pace/timing. Do you speak too quickly to be fully understood or too slowly to be interesting and hold attention? Nervous novice instructors often speak too quickly. Veteran instructors know the value of slowing down, even pausing now and then for emphasis and assimilation. A few well-chosen words spoken slowly and clearly usually leaves a more lasting impression than a breathless stream of unbroken syllables.

Word choice. Big and obscure words are wasted if your students don't understand them. Choose a simple clear vocabulary which everyone can follow. Generally, the simpler the better.

When using nautical terminology or technical jargon, be sure to define each term as you go along. If you are not positive every student recalls terms previously defined, pause to repeat their definition. Some students are understandably shy about speaking up to confess their ignorance of a term. Don't risk losing your audience by carelessly assuming they share your vocabulary.

Avoid verbal excesses such as guttural pauses (e.g. 'ums' and 'ers') and stale, trite or overused expressions. They usually distract more than they contribute to the lesson.

The purpose/value statement is a teaching tool. It is a brief opening remark designed to capture the students' attention. **Students are more likely to pay attention if they perceive some benefit**. So it is helpful when introducing a new topic to begin by stating its purpose and value to the students.

Briefly ask and answer the questions:
"What is this for?"
"What good is it?"

A topic which has no purpose or value need not be in a curriculum. An instructor who cannot clearly state the **purpose and value** of a subject matter is probably not prepared to teach it.

Every topic should have purpose and value.

Non-Verbal Communication

People unconsciously communicate without words all the time. What people verbalize is only part of the communication process. Non-verbal communication includes everything about you *other than* your spoken words, which contributes to what and how your message is received by your students.

Presence Your students, almost certainly, will size you up as soon as they first meet you to decide if they are comfortable submitting to your leadership. A confident, deliberate, and enthusiastic appearance will get you started on the right foot. Stand up straight, keep your head up, stay focused, look people in the eye, be well organized, speak clearly, and take charge.

Gestures can work for you or against you. If your gestures are meaningful and clearly help amplify your point, by all means use them. If they are just excess motion or a nervous habit, however, they are a distraction and should be avoided. The eye is naturally drawn to motion. If there is no useful message in your gestures, don't let them draw visual attention away from a more productive part of the lesson.

Body language. How you hold your body can work for you or against you as well. Your posture conveys implied messages about your mood and attitude. Crossed arms or legs suggest defensiveness. A cocked head suggests skepticism or defiance. Leaning forward in a chair or standing too close may suggest assertiveness or aggression. Your total appearance determines how your students will respond to you. For a positive response project a friendly open image. Be body conscious.

Eye contact is a powerful teaching tool. It not only concentrates and focuses the attention of the student, it supplies the instructor with valuable feedback. Eyes reveal confusion or understanding, excitement or boredom, confidence or insecurity. They tell the instructor when and how to adjust the pace and teaching technique to the needs of the moment. Students need to see your eyes too. They should not be hidden behind sunglasses while classroom teaching. Use sunglasses only in on-the-water instruction.

Attitude. Your facial expressions, body language, tone of voice, general demeanor, behavior, and choice of words all add up to a reflection of your attitude. If it inspires your students, it works in your favor. If it turns them off or disillusions them, it works against you, Think often and carefully about all the subtle messages you send to others about yourself. Remember, you are a role model.

See yourself as others may see you.
Is your appearance interfering with learning?

Mixed signals are usually the result of carelessness. Mixed signals send opposing messages and create confusion. If you to say, "watch your step," while pointing upwards, a student would not know which way to look, up or down. If you advise your students to use a 3-point stance and step to the center of the hull when boarding, then later you leap onto the bow, your students will notice the contradiction and be confused. Your words and example do not agree. Whether in the classroom or on the water, be sure all of your communication tools are sending a consistent, clear, unambiguous message. Live what you preach every day.

Mannerisms are behavioral excesses which are usually distracting. They include such nervous habits as pacing, jingling pocket change, tapping a pen, drumming fingers on a desk, or any other repetitive and unproductive behavior. None contribute to the message, and all are distracting to your students.

Teaching New Skills

A student normally passes through three general phases in acquiring a new skill: *learning,* *consolidation,* and *automatic.*

1. **In the *learning phase,*** the student simply learns to perform the simple sequential steps involved in carrying out a more complex physical skill, such as tacking. The instructor may wish to introduce the skill in its broader context in a classroom setting at first. There it can be established when and why the skill is used. Analogies are helpful in the learning phase, so a student may relate new ideas to something familiar. Then the instructor divides the new skill into its smallest elementary steps. Each step is described and demonstrated in its proper sequence before the students try it for themselves.

Slow motion walk-throughs or *land drills* are helpful at first, because they incorporate a kinesthetic element to the instruction and provide more assimilation time than a real life tack. Whenever a skill is completely new to the student, it is important to slow the pace and provide nearly constant step by step feedback and encouragement. As the student catches on, the pace of the simulated tacks can be accelerated gradually until they reach "real time," actual speed. Then the student is ready to perform a "real" tack.

> ☞ **INSTRUCTORS TAKE NOTE...**
> *Land Drills* are important when introducing a new skill.

An instructor may spot several errors in the student's first efforts but should resist the temptation to blurt them all out at once. Keep it simple. Using the *criticism sandwich,* first find something to praise, then zero in on the correction. In general, focus on only one error at a time, with the most important first. Always end with an encouraging word. Positive reinforcement is very important in sustaining motivation in the learning phase. Be patient and enthusiastic.

Plenty of praise and encouragement is the order of the day in the learning phase.

The type of critical feedback an instructor should offer during the learning phase depends on whether mistakes are *learning* or *performance* errors.

A *learning error* is a mistake due to a misunderstanding of the correct way to perform a skill. For example, a student who mistakenly pushes the tiller to leeward in order to jibe, may not have understood which way to move the tiller from the outset. If so, it is a learning error. In such a case the instructor needs to review or repeat the original instruction on how to jibe correctly.

> ☞ **INSTRUCTORS TAKE NOTE...**
> Focus on teaching essential core skills until students are near to mastery before you address lower priority technical improvements.

A *performance error* is not a mistake of understanding, rather one of execution. A student who oversteers in a jibe may understand the correct steps involved in jibing but needs only to refine their execution. Appropriate feedback, therefore, would be a simple *criticism sandwich* rather than a full repetition of the original lesson on how to jibe.

Whether correcting a performance or a learning error, an instructor should be alert and respond promptly. Correction feedback should be immediate whenever possible, so a mistake does not get a chance to become a habit. A mistake undetected is a mistake uncorrected.

2. **In the *consolidation phase*,** the student practices merging each step into a single smooth coordinated maneuver, and may need only occasional correction and encouragement.

In this second phase a motivated student may become so completely absorbed in the challenge of performance that his or her awareness and concentration level reaches a peak. This is a critical period where the student is learning by doing, experimenting, and to some extent, self-correcting and even self-reinforcing.

In the consolidation phase, learning takes place mostly kinesthetically and visually. While practicing the new skill, the student receives steady instant feedback simply by feeling and observing the consequences (tiller and sheet pressure, wind and hull velocity changes, heel changes, amount of luff, etc.) of his/her actions. Feeling and observing the fluctuations of all the variables is a critical part of learning to sail. Repetitions build channels of kinesthetic memory so that complex skills are gradually performed more smoothly, with less awkwardness and hesitation.

> ☞ **INSTRUCTORS TAKE NOTE...**
> *Water Drills* are an important teaching tool in this consolidation phase.

Refrain from unnecessarily interrupting this valuable learning-by-doing process with excessive feedback. Students should not be prevented from making all mistakes. Experiencing the consequences of performance errors is a vital and productive part of learning to sail. Unless there is physical danger or you see a learning error, be patient. Simply observe from a non-distracting distance until your comments are truly needed.

Don't overdo feedback or try to prevent all mistakes.
Sometimes it's best to cork it!

3. **In the *automatic phase*,** full skill execution starts to click. The student understands what is required and performs the maneuver consistently and competently. This is a confidence building period which then paves the way to the next skill in the lesson plan.

When To Stop Talking. While some instructors may offer too little feedback to their students, others talk too much. An instructor who talks too much at the wrong time is more of a distraction and a pest than a help.

One such time for an instructor to be sparing with words is during *overload*. A student experiences *overload* when there is too much happening too quickly for the student to assimilate any more input. During the commotion of a sudden round-up following an accidental flying jibe, for example, is not the best moment for a barrage of feedback. When a student is fully occupied with the demands of the moment, feedback probably will not be heard or remembered. Unless there is danger, wait for such a hectic situation to stabilize before beginning instructive feedback.

Direct vs. Indirect Commands. "Pull the tiller toward you" is a direct command. A *direct command* requests a simple explicit action without inferring its consequence or intended result.

"Bear off" is an indirect command. An *indirect command* presumes that the student understands what intermediate steps are required (i.e., where to move the tiller) and focuses rather on the intended result.

Indirect commands are verbal short-cuts. They save the instructor time and words. They may be used as long as the student is appropriately responsive. But if the student appears confused or balks, the instructor may need to revert to simpler direct commands. Beginners often need mostly direct commands until they become accustomed to performing routine maneuvers and are familiar with proper terminology.

☞ **INSTRUCTORS TAKE NOTE...**
- A **direct command** is very explicit and is appropriate when a beginner is confused or is having trouble understanding technical terms.
- An **indirect command** is a communication short-cut, useful with more experienced students. It requests a desired result without specifying a method to achieve it.

Ambiguity in your choice of words may create confusion between a direct and an indirect command.

Being Heard. An instructor should be aware of obstructions or impediments to voice communication. Don't try to talk to a student through a sail or other object. If you can't see the student's ears, there is a poor chance you will be heard clearly. Avoid competing with other loud sounds such as a luffing sail, engine noise, or an airplane passing over-head. Wait for a lull. Your message is more likely to be heard clearly and in its entirety.

Don't try to talk through a sail.
If you can't see their ears, they probably won't hear you.

Being Seen. Visual communication techniques, such as gestures and hand signals, are best used when the student can easily see them without distraction from the central task. When the instructor monitors from the backstay, typical of keelboat instruction, visual signals may go unnoticed because the instructor is outside of the students' field of view. When being seen is necessary for effective communication, the instructor should move to the cockpit.

When teaching from a safety boat, the instructor should position the safety boat ahead and slightly to windward of the student's vessel. From that position the student can see hand signals or gestures with a simple glance rather than a head turn.

Being seen and heard together, of course, is the most effective way to communicate on the water. Gestures amplify a spoken message by repeating it visually, and gestures provide backup for any words lost in wind or engine noise.

See "Safety and You" in Section 2 of the *Small Boat Sailing Level 1 Instructor Manual* for additional information on Visual Signals.

Teaching vs. Coaching

When teaching a new skill an instructor must be patient, methodical, and very encouraging. High quality performance is not the object when learning a new skill. Simply imprinting the sequence of the individual component steps of a maneuver is the initial mission (the learning phase). Once the student can reliably perform the maneuver (the automatic phase), however awkwardly, coaching takes over from teaching.

Coaching is a training regimen geared toward improving existing skills more so than learning brand new ones. Teaching and coaching techniques are quite similar, but they are different in one important aspect. In coaching, the instructor generally employs an intermittent positive reinforcement schedule, rather than a regular one. That is, by selectively reinforcing a behavior, the instructor can gradually raise the stakes, shaping performance by praising only improved performance rather than mere adequacy. The student is encouraged to improve performance by the instructor's increasingly higher standards and expectations.

LEADERSHIP

The Role of a Role Model

Because an instructor is an authority figure, students are constantly influenced by his or her opinions, judgment, and behavior. It comes with the territory.

Responsible instructors should be quite conscious of the appropriateness of their behavior, so they do not inadvertently set a poor example, and so they can serve as effective role models. Students, particularly younger ones, often want and need role models to set a standard of behavior and performance. If instructors live up to high professional standards, they will naturally earn their students' respect. Once they have their students' respect they are in a position to be effective as leaders, teachers, and coaches.

Leadership Styles

Sailing instructors are as different from one another as sailing students. Each has a unique personality, and each develops a unique personal teaching style. It is important to develop a comfortable and natural style, but be careful to avoid some of the pitfalls. Some instructors adopt leadership styles which serve their own interests better than those of their students.

Authoritarian Style.
The Authoritarian Style is characterized by an autocratic and firm attitude. This style is often necessary in situations where the safety of the students, sailors, and boats is at risk. But avoid unnecessary or exaggerated use of this style. You may be perceived as a "Dictator." The *Dictator* is a domineering personality who insists on making all the decisions and giving orders. The Dictator rarely listens to the students or involves them in any decision making regarding their instruction.

The Authoritarian Style

Wimp Style. At the other end of the leadership scale is the Wimp Style. The *Wimp* is unsure and submissive and has difficulty making even minor decisions. The Wimp is a pushover who yields too easily in order to avoid conflict. The Wimp may be perceived as spineless for failing to take firm charge when the situation warrants. The Wimp is not well respected by his students, so they do not take his orders seriously.

The Wimp Style is the opposite extreme from the Authoritarian Style. It shows no leadership control at all.

Cooperative Style. The Cooperative Style of leadership is characterized by teamwork. It is a delicate balance of solid independent leadership and thoughtful student consultation. The Cooperative instructor neither dictates nor wimps out. The Cooperative instructor encourages student involvement in decision making, listens carefully and fairly, and maintains control without needlessly asserting authority over the students. The Cooperative instructor favors positive leadership skills rather than arrogance or autonomy.

In general, US SAILING encourages instructors to use the Cooperative Style. Nevertheless, they also should be able to shift quickly to the Authoritarian Style when it is the most effective way to safeguard their students' safety. The challenge for instructors is recognizing *when* the Authoritarian Style is justified and necessary, and *how* to avoid overusing it.

Characteristics of a Leader

Trustworthiness and respect are key ingredients to leadership. A trusted and respected instructor can lift morale and inspire students to outstanding accomplishment. It is only natural for people to want to please or impress people whom they respect or admire.

Conversely, it is only natural for people to be indifferent to those for whom they have no respect. Instructors who fail to live up to their duty as a role model earn little respect from their students. Without the students' respect, motivation suffers, and an instructor can accomplish very little.

Respect does not come automatically with the job title. It must be earned every day. The wise instructor works to earn respect right at the outset of the student/instructor relationship. It is a critical period for developing motivation and good morale.

Students are more apt to accept an instructor's leadership if they feel they are in good hands. That requires some initial trust-building through clearly stated goals, a realistic plan, and an enthusiastic positive attitude.

If you ask students to list the most admirable qualities of people they truly respect, you would hear many of the same characteristics again and again. People respect those who are dedicated, competent, trustworthy, dependable, determined, unselfish, courageous, honest, and have clear and worthy goals and unyielding principles.

If you want to get the job done well, you need to be a good leader. If you want to be a good leader, you have to be trusted and respected. If you want to be trusted and respected, you have to live up to the standards of your duty as a role model. How successful you are largely depends on how well you measure up to the above characteristics.

Goal Setting

Part of good leadership is establishing clear and attainable goals. Goals need to be stated at the outset to help initiate student motivation. Students are more likely to put their all into an effort, if they clearly understand and agree with the intended result before they begin. Students naturally feel more enthusiastic knowing that their leader has a realistic plan with clearly defined steps.

*Setting goals and marking progress
provide inspiration and encouragement.*

Goal setting should involve both long and short term goals. Short term goals are stepping stones toward higher achievement. Short term goals are important to motivation. They provide intermediate opportunities for success. Frequent success is positively reinforcing and encourages ongoing motivation. Short term goals can be quite modest, perhaps as simple as daily checklist accomplishments. They serve as encouraging reminders to students that they are making daily progress toward the more difficult long term goals.

Taking Charge

An essential duty of any leader is taking charge and giving orders. Students want and need to know what they should be doing. They look to their leader, the instructor, for direction. Students soon lose patience and confidence in leadership which appears confused or uncertain.

Organize yourself *before* class. Have a well defined plan of what you want from a class and then communicate it clearly.

***When it's time to take charge,
be organized, clear and specific.***

When it is time for decisive action, give direct orders, not suggestions or requests. Direct orders need not be arrogant or abrasive, they simply need to be specific and unambiguous. When it is appropriate to use the Authoritarian style of leadership, use a command voice. Speak simply, clearly, unequivocally, and with a firm command tone. Look your students squarely in the eye when issuing orders. Follow the four W's:

1. Who
2. What
3. When
4. Where

Example: "Dale, get a couple of PFDs from the locker; and meet me at the rigging dock in ten minutes."

You cannot expect specific results if your orders are vague and unspecific. "Somebody get a bucket," for example, does not address anyone in particular, so it may get no response at all.

Listening Skills

Because teaching is a two-way communication process, where teacher and student provide feedback to one another, listening well is vital. An instructor should listen well, interrupt only to clarify, and pause to think carefully before responding.

When a student asks a question in a classroom setting, good active listening involves repeating the question for the benefit of the other students who may not have heard, then, after answering, asking if the response fully answers the question. Conscientiously responding to student questions and concerns builds trust and strengthens respect.

Good active listening also sometimes requires discerning the "real message" buried in the words. A student who offers frequent weak excuses, for example, may be masking a totally different hidden concern. Excuses are often indicators of avoidance behavior.

Team Building

Team building involves building bonds between members of a group. In group instruction it is an important responsibility. The instructor is the group leader and catalyst for student relations. Good morale and a cooperative spirit among classmates can greatly enhance the teaching environment and learning outcome. Break the ice early among new students. Make introductions right away so that no one feels they are among strangers. Have them engage in games, exercises or social activities which require interaction and cooperation.

Much of the team building process takes place naturally as new students get to know one another. The instructor should be a facilitator not a focal point in the process. Gradually, as familiarity and trust develop, communication, teamwork and morale grow. An instructor should monitor group morale and employ team building exercises as often as needed to keep the learning experience fun and productive.

Discipline

Controlling student mis-behavior is not ordinarily an issue when teaching adults, yet it is nearly an everyday occurrence when teaching children.

Since

**safety,
fun and
learning**

are unalterable components of an instructor's mission, no individual student's behavior should be allowed to deprive the rest of the class from reaching these goals.

SAFETY, FUN AND LEARNING MUST BE MAINTAINED!

The learning environment must be fun and safe to be effective. Don't let unruly students ruin it for others.

Prevention. An instructor can prevent most behavior problems by doing three things:

1. State clearly and firmly the rules of conduct on the very first day of instruction.
2. Maintain a well structured lesson plan and learning environment.
3. Keep the students busy -- no idle time.

Young sailors with immature social skills, high energy levels, and limited self-discipline generally require more structure in their learning environment than adults. A busy student who is constantly engaged in constructive activity has little time and opportunity to get into mischief. A well-organized and highly constructive daily lesson plan should provide nearly seamless continuity from one activity to the next with very little idle time.

When behavior does go awry, it is important that the instructor not overreact and that the response be proportionate to the offense.

Redirection. In mild cases of misbehavior, such as simple inattention, the student may only need to be *redirected*. Redirecting is bringing the errant student to attention and refocusing him or her on the task at hand.

Extinction. Recurring mischievous or disruptive behavior is sometimes an over anxious student's way of seeking the instructor's attention. If so, it is sometimes best handled by extinction, that is, by simply ignoring it. Ignoring the student's antics denies him or her the positive reinforcement of the instructor's attention. Without positive reinforcement the student's undesirable behavior may become less frequent and eventually cease without further action.

Increasing Responsibility. Another technique is to invite a student to assist in conducting the class. Sometimes giving mischievous students some responsibility (such as supervising clean-up, or helping to teach younger students) is all that is needed to instill pride, bring them onto the team, and provide them with needed positive motivation.

> ☞ **INSTRUCTORS TAKE NOTE...**
> Some measures to consider in controlling student behavior:
> 1. Prevention
> 2. Redirection (refocus attention)
> 3. Extinction (ignore it)
> 4. Increase responsibility
> 5. Punishment
> 6. Suspension
> 7. Expulsion

Punishment. Harmful or dangerous excesses in a student's behavior, which must be curtailed immediately, may need to be controlled with punishment. Punishment may take the form of a stern reprimand or, in more serious cases, perhaps a suspension of privileges. Chronic misconduct should be brought to the attention of the student's parents, since it may indicate a more deep-seated problem requiring their involvement. See -- "Parents in a Junior Sailing Program" in the *Developing a Program Curriculum* section of this manual for further discussion.

It should be noted that a shortcoming of punishment is that it can cause more problems than it solves by inadvertently extinguishing otherwise desirable behavior. A public reprimand, for instance, may do more than halt childish antics. It may dampen an adolescent's motivation and trigger a defensive response. If an instructor overreacts to the offense, a single minor instance of misbehavior could evolve into an ongoing pattern of withdrawal or defiance. As a rule, punishment should be used sparingly and generally only as a last resort. As the saying goes, "you catch more flies with honey..."

Suspension/Expulsion. Incorrigible and dangerous misconduct which jeopardizes anyone's safety, consistently disrupts the teaching environment, or seriously damages the morale of the other students must be controlled decisively. If a student's persistently unruly behavior cannot be brought under control by one or more of the above measures, it may be necessary to consider suspension or even permanent expulsion.

SECTION 2

CURRICULUM DEVELOPMENT

Sample Forms and Guidelines

CURRICULUM DEVELOPMENT

Normally, Small Boat Sailing Level 1 Instructors are not responsible for planning and developing a program curriculum. This is usually done by a program organizer and/or the program director/head instructor. However, understanding the process will help you to implement the curriculum and prepare lesson plans.

A Process for Curriculum Development

Curriculum Overview of Program. The curriculum for any instructional program is a cursory summation of all courses offered within a program and the major topics covered in each course. Designing a curriculum requires that the planner determine which courses will be offered in a program and then specify their relation to each other. Integrating each sailing course into a cohesive program to enhance program flow is the ultimate goal of curriculum planning. **A good curriculum allows a program planner to integrate the subject matter of all the sailing courses to form a logical progression from one course level to the next, emphasizing the *building block approach*.** The progression of courses should increase in complexity and content to match the ability and skill of the students, yet also strive to review previous skills. It might be helpful to create a flow chart (see sample one several pages later) to diagram the progression from one course level to the next. Visualizing how the courses relate to each other allows for an easier understanding of how topics for each course are related, aiding the curriculum planner in designing a cohesive program of instruction.

☑ **Imagination and Innovation.** It is not as if there is only one correct method for teaching a subject. An instructor must take into account his or her own teaching strengths and weaknesses, and more importantly the needs of the students. **Dare to be creative.** Very often the best lessons are those that are completely unique from any other. Additionally, most people develop a better understanding of new material if they can relate it to something they already understand. If you can help students to make such connections, your job will be easier. Consider the best and most memorable lessons you have had. Why are those lessons so lasting in your memory?

When developing a curriculum (or lesson plans) think in terms of what it will be like for the students. Always try to put yourself in their shoes. While this planning process will require more time to develop, your teaching will rise to its greatest potential.

Time Frame Considerations

It's never easy to place any teaching program into a time frame. There will always be less time than you need, and more skills that you would like to teach. Your job as an instructor is to give *each* student as much exposure as possible to active instruction ashore and afloat. **The framework for designing a program curriculum is coordination between the number of instruction hours available and the number of students in each class.** Your most difficult task is deciding whether each skill will take a long or short time for the average student to master, or assessing your students' ability.

☑ **Pace.** To simplify your task, research previous lesson plans and student evaluations as a guideline and reference. In general, strike a balance between going slow enough for everyone to master a skill and rushing ahead so quickly that students don't understand how to perform the skills. In teaching skills correctly the first time, you will not necessarily be able to guarantee that every student can actually perform the skill. Rather, each student should understand *how* to perform the skill and understand the areas they need to improve for mastery of the skill. It is, however, more important to give beginning students more time to learn and master basic skills before progressing to more advanced skills and catering to advanced students.

☑ **Total Hours.** Your first task in creating a curriculum is to determine the total hours available for each class, taking into account all the days that the students will be away on vacation, racing, field trips, etc. As a guide, an average student needs approximately 14 to 30 hours of instruction, depending on age and ability, to master the skills for US SAILING's Small Boat Sailor Certification.

Essential Ingredients

The three most important objectives in creating a curriculum and subsequent lesson plans are **SAFETY, FUN and LEARNING.** Safety and learning are obvious, but all too often fun is left out. Designing a course that includes fun is not only more enjoyable, but also enhances and facilitates learning. (See "Games --Teaching the Fun Way" in Section 2.) In other words, most people learn best when they don't even realize that they are learning, but are merely enjoying an activity. **Several keys to a fun sailing course are:**

☑ **Diversity.** Repetitive activities soon become boring and dull. By teaching through varied activities you will keep classes fresh and exciting.

☑ **Organization.** There are few things that are more frustrating than a lack of organization. Not only does it appear unprofessional, but loose ends and complications make the learning process more difficult for all students. This is why US SAILING advocates using the building block method of instruction. The *building block method* is where each course and each lesson are linked together to maximize flow and continuity in subject matter. Prior planning is absolutely essential for efficient integration of subject matter.

☑ **Pace.** Creating an overall curriculum and designing a course outline will be instrumental in budgeting your time as an instructor. A **timetable** for the course you teach will ultimately help each instructor to plan an adequate amount of time for each topic or skill. In addition, if **you teach things correctly the first time** you will not only avoid having to teach them again, but you will be able to build on top of the foundation of knowledge you have already established! Breaking incorrect habits down the road is far more difficult and time consuming than teaching skills properly the first time around.

☑ **Local Conditions.** You must also take into account prevailing weather patterns. Is it light wind in the morning building up to a fresh breeze, or the reverse? If your sailing site is tidal and you can only sail so many hours around high tide, that too must be considered. You have to decide when it is best to schedule each class so that students can maximize their learning time by practicing during weather conditions within their abilities.

☑ **Class/Session Time.** Again as a guide, aim at a minimum of three hours of instruction for a session. Even then, a large portion of class time is going to be taken up with rigging boats and getting to the sailing area. When planning the length of each class session, take into consideration:

- The attention span of the students
- The difficulty of the skills students will be learning
- The goals and activities of each course
- The length of the sailing season
- The format of your program
- Other activities and obligations of your students

✎ TIME ALLOCATION AND CURRICULUM PLANNING...
The most important aspect of time allocation and curriculum planning is making sure that you do not try to cover too much information. If you create a schedule where the students must absorb more than 2-3 primary concepts per class, you will probably be teaching over their heads and beyond their ability. This is especially true of beginning sailors where every skill and idea is new to them. Keeping things simple in the allocated time will allow more students to master skills and information so they will feel successful and want to learn more.

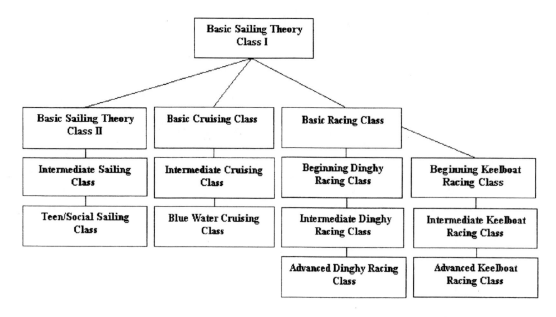

Curriculum Development of Course. After deciding on the number of classes or courses to be taught and the time frame of each class, the program planner should develop:

- **Course Outlines**
- **Course Content**
- **A Weekly Syllabus for each course**
- **Lesson Plans** (the course instructor should ultimately take responsibility for writing lesson plans)

Course Outline

The course outline serves as a rough guide for the skills and information to be taught in each course. When combined together, the course outlines will provide the structure for the whole program curriculum. A course outline should take into account the program goals and the ability level of the students in each course. Furthermore, a course outline should organize topic areas so that they utilize the *building block method* of instruction by starting with essential skills and progressing to complex or combined skills. (*See sample later in this section.*)

Course Content

The course content is an elaboration of the course outline, specifically identifying the topics and skills to be taught in each sailing course. To begin development of course content, place all the topics for instruction in your program on a list progressing from basic skills to complex skills. In essence, the list is a sequence of topics for study from beginner groups to advanced and specialized groups. While each course should have its own topics of study, there should be some overlap in topics to facilitate a smooth progression in courses. Course content, as an elaboration on the skills specific to each class, should follow the course outline. Instruction should begin with essential skills (i.e. starting, stopping, tacking) and work toward combining unrelated skills into a new skill (i.e. overboard recovery) at more advanced levels of instruction. (*See sample later in this section.*)

Syllabus

The syllabus is either a whole course or weekly list of the topics to be covered in your sailing class on any given date. An instructor should use the syllabus to:

- create flow and continuity from class to class, and
- as a broad outline for each lesson plan (including activities for each class).

A smart instructor will create a syllabus for the entire course to properly budget his or her time on each topic or skill and to create a consistent pace for the course.

Lesson Plans

When developing lesson plans, keep the pace lively and use a variety of activities each day -- diversity in your activities will keep students involved and interactive. Refer to your syllabus to locate the topic(s) for any day, then plan activities and methods of instruction that will best convey information to your students. You should try to plan one goal for the day, preparing not more than 2-3 central concepts from that goal. You may find that it is necessary to supply students with supplemental information, or *secondary* concepts, to support the 2-3 *central* concepts of your lesson. The secondary concepts elaborate on, and help to explain the central concepts of your lessons, just like the supporting cast of a play or movie elaborates on the plot.

> **✎ A PLANNING TIP...**
> In a worst case scenario, you may have to delay your detailed planning until you have conducted a couple of classes for assessment of your students.

There are a number of ways to prepare lesson plans, but whatever format you use it should include the following:

- The daily goal
- The general areas covered (central concepts)
- The activities
- Time for each activity
- The method used to instruct each activity
- The equipment needs for the class

Remember that your lesson plans must be detailed enough for other instructors to use. In the event that you are unable to teach a class (i.e. field trips, other activities or duties, illness) another instructor will probably have to take your place, just like a substitute teacher. **A complete and detailed class plan will keep your class outline on target and produce the goals you set when you wrote the lesson.**

> *The following Sailing Program samples have been taken from various programs across the United States to provide a greater representation of methods, techniques, and styles. Due to the range of the samples, the content information is not intended to flow or coincide from one example to the next.*

Basic Sailing Beginner

GOAL: To become a safe and independent Sabot sailor and to pass a swim test

CLASS TOPIC AREAS AND REQUIRED OUTCOMES:

MANEUVERS AFLOAT (wind up to 10 mph)
1. Get safely in and out of a Sabot.
2. Independently rig and derig a Sabot.
3. With a team, flip a Sabot and put on a rack.
4. Perform the following maneuvers with instructor supervision:
   - ☑ Sail on a beat, reach, and run.
   - ☑ Tack and jibe.
   - ☑ Beach, dock and sail off from each.
   - ☑ Tie onto a tow.
   - ☑ Get out of irons.

TERMINOLOGY
1. Boat: hull, bow, stern, port, starboard, sail, tack, clew, head, mast, boom, rudder, tiller, leeboard, main sheet, downhaul, outhaul
2. Sailing: tack, jibe, close-hauled, reaching, running

SAFETY AWARENESS
1. Show how to put on and secure a PFD properly while in the water.
2. Sail into and out of the "Safety Position and describe uses for "Safety Position."
3. Demonstrate capsize and crew overboard rescue.
4. Explain why wearing shoes at the facility is a requirement and good idea.

RULES
1. State the first rule of sailing -- (render assistance).
2. Describe when and how to check for other boats.
3. Tell why and how to avoid a collision.

MAINTENANCE
1. Demonstrate how to store the boat and equipment after sailing.
2. Show how to roll, fold, or store a sail after sailing.
3. Wash the boat and equipment properly.
4. Help in 2 facility work projects (trash pick-up, facility-Sabot inspection & wash).

SEAMANSHIP KNOWLEDGE
1. State the difference between a rope, a line, and a sheet.
2. Tie a figure-8 knot, square knot, two half hitches, and bowline and discuss their uses.
3. Secure a boat to a dock with a cleat hitch.

ENVIRONMENTAL AWARENESS
1. Identify wind direction on land and name three ways to tell wind direction.
2. Describe weather and water clues that indicate good or bad sailing conditions.
3. Define water pollution and list two ways sailors can help the environment.

GENERAL SAILING KNOWLEDGE
I. Identify the insignia of a Naples Sabot.
2. Describe the difference between a monohull and a multihull and name one boat of each kind.
3. State three main uses of recreational boats.

EVALUATION AND CLASS PARTY

Basic Sailing Beginner

WEATHER, WIND AND CURRENT
- Sensing Wind Direction: visual, tactile
- Predicting Puffs and Lulls: water surface

KNOTS
- Types of Line
- Bowline
- Figure-8
- Cleat Hitch
- Two Half Hitches
- Rolling Hitch
- Coiling a Line
- Heaving a Line

BOATHANDLING
- Stopping and Starting
- Safety Position
- Reaching: *weight placement, sail trim, steering, centerboard, puffs and lulls*
- Close-hauled: *weight placement, hiking, sail trim, steering, centerboard, puffs and lulls*
- Running: *weight placement, sail trim, steering, centerboard*
- Tacking: *steering, use of tiller extension, smooth cross-over, hand exchange, sail trim, commands*
- Jibing: *controlled jibe, steering, smooth cross-over, hand exchange, sail trim, commands*
- Docking: *departure and landing (into the wind)*

RULES
- Basic Right-of-Way
- Emergency Procedures
- Overboard Recovery

SEAMANSHIP
- Rigging and De-rigging
- Basic Navigation: buoy system, channels
- Boat Care
- Sail Care
- Parts of the Boat
- Parts of the Sail
- Anchoring
- Towing

Basic Sailing Beginner

FORMAT: (8) three-hour lessons for youth or adults for one week or several weeks

CLASS I

TOPIC	TIME ALLOWANCE
Introduction and Course Overview	10 minutes
Team Building	15 minutes
Tour of Facility	15 minutes
Life Jackets - Inspection, Sizing and Lecture	10 minutes
Swim Test Lecture	5 minutes
Swim Test Actual Practical Test	30 minutes
Capsize Recovery - *SSR!* Video Segment 5 and Demonstration	15 minutes
Capsize Recovery Practice	45 minutes
Basic Knots - *SSR!* Video Segment 3	30 minutes
Debrief	5 minutes

CLASS 2

Topic	Time Allowance
Introduction/Review	15 minutes
Weather Lecture	20 minutes
Safe Sailing Lecture and *SSR!* Video Segment 1	15 minutes
Rigging Boats Demonstration	5 minutes
Rigging Boats Practice	25 minutes
First Sail Lecture and *SSR!* Video Segment 9	15 minutes
First Sail on the Water Practice	55 minutes
De-Rigging Boats	25 minutes
Debrief	5 minutes

CLASS 3

Topic	Time Allowance
Introduction/Review	5 minutes
Wind Lecture and Land Drills	15 minutes
Basic Sailing Maneuvers - Steering and Tacking	15 minutes
Rigging Boats	25 minutes
On the Water Practice	90 minutes
De-Rigging Boats	20 minutes
Weather Review	5 minutes
Debrief	5 minutes

CLASS 4

Topic	Time Allowance
Introduction/Review	5 minutes
How a Sailboat Sails Lecture and *SSR!* Video Segment 4	10 minutes
Tacking Lecture and Land Drills	15 minutes
Rigging Boats	25 minutes
On the Water Practice	90 minutes
De-Rigging Boats	20 minutes
Knot Relay Race	10 minutes
Debrief	5 minutes

CLASS 5

Topic	Time Allowance
Introduction/Review	10 minutes
Jibing Lecture and Land Drills	15 minutes
Rigging Boats	15 minutes
Hand Signals	10 minutes
On the Water Practice including Capsize Drill	90 minutes
De-Rigging Boats	15 minutes
Right-of-Way Lecture, *SSR!* Video Segment 13 and Land Drill	20 minutes
Debrief	5 minutes

CLASS 6

Topic	Time Allowance
Introduction/Review	5 minutes
Steering Upwind and Use of Telltales	20 minutes
Rigging Boats	15 minutes
On the Water Practice	90 minutes
Docking Practice	30 minutes
De-Rigging Boats	15 minutes
Debrief	5 minutes

CLASS 7

Topic	Time Allowance
Introduction/Review	5 minutes
Overboard Recovery Lecture, *SSR!* Video Segment 6 and Land Drills	30 minutes
Rigging Boats	15 minutes
On the Water Practice	90 minutes
De-Rigging Boats	15 minutes
Relay Race	20 minutes
Debrief	5 minutes

CLASS 8

Topic	Time Allowance
Introduction/Review	5 minutes
Rigging Boats	15 minutes
On the Water Practice	90 minutes
De-Rigging Boats	15 minutes
Review of Land Skills, Oral Review and Written Test	30 minutes

SAMPLE: LESSON PLAN #1

Basic Sailing Beginner

LESSON PLAN FOR: _Beginner 420_____   DATE: Monday
LESSON NUMBER: ___1___

OBJECTIVE/GOAL: basic knots, nomenclature, rig/derig, swim and scoop
    a) acquaint students with basic knots
    b) parts of the boats
    c) rigging and de-rigging
    d) scoop recovery and swim test

MATERIALS:
    1 rigged 420   1 de-rigged 420
    Class notebooks   1 safety boat
    Lines for knot tying

CONTENT:
  Review: ---

  Material Introduction:
    boat nomenclature, scoop recovery, and knots

  Methods/Activities:
    (30 min.) Land Drill: basic knot demonstration and practice of bowline and figure-8

    (40 min.) Land Demonstration: a) proper rigging of 420, b) de-rigging and proper storage of 420, c) scoop recovery

    (40 min.) Water Drill: administer swim test and scoop recovery. Students test two at a time, and then demonstrate scoop recovery on moored boat before getting out of water.

    (40 min) Water Drill: students steering boat being towed -- no sails. Each student takes turn as skipper and crew. Develop feel for stability and helm reaction.

  Closure:
    (20 min.) Review parts of the boat, and pass out nomenclature handout for notebooks.

REMARKS/COMMENTS:
Students had full day with information overload. Towing worked well as a means of developing student comfort in the boats and increasing their confidence.

TCF 2/9   2-13

SAMPLE: LESSON PLAN #2

Basic Sailing Beginner

LESSON PLAN FOR: _Beginner 420_____   DATE: Tuesday
LESSON NUMBER: __2___

OBJECTIVE/GOAL: sailing on a reach
    a) have students understand basic rigging of a 420 main & jib
    b) students properly adjust sails and helm while sailing on a reach
    c) students tack the boat in Figure-8 drill

MATERIALS:
    Whiteboard & markers   3 de-rigged 420s
    2 drop buoys   1 safety boat

CONTENT:
Review:
    knots: bowline, Figure-8
    parts of boat & sail

Material Introduction:
    safety position, tacking & reaching for Figure-8 Water Drill

Methods/Activities:
(20 min.) Chalk talk on: a) no-go zone for docking & stopping; b) tacking, reaching and Figure-8 Water Drill pattern; c) safety position if necessary on the water.

(30 min.) Practice for students as they rig boats.

(20 min.) Water Drill as students depart 420 float to immediate practice of the safety position.

(40 min.) Water Drill as students sail from practice of safety position drill to Figure-8 drill. Provide on-the-water coaching for sail adjustments and tacking practice.

(30 min) Practice for students as they de-rig the 420s making sure boats are secured and sails/equipment are properly stowed away.

Closure:
(20 min.) Review no-go zone and docking, body positions in boat, Figure-8 drill, safety position, and individual evaluations of strong points and areas for improvement.

REMARKS/COMMENTS:
Sailing from boat float allowed for reaching in all segments of water drills. Figure-8 drill works well because it is a point and go pattern -- students just have to aim for the mark and push tiller towards sail.

TCF 2/9

Basic Sailing Beginner

LESSON PLAN FOR: _Beginner 420_____ DATE: Wednesday
LESSON NUMBER: __3___

OBJECTIVE/GOAL: reaching and sail adjustment
  a) reinforce student confidence and comfort in the boat
  b) reinforce proper body position and use of weight
  c) continue practicing sail adjustment on reaches and tacking

MATERIALS:
  Whiteboard & markers   3 de-rigged 420s
  2 drop buoys   1 safety boat

CONTENT:
  Review:
    safety position and tacking
    remind students of dangers from open automatic bailers during capsize
      recovery

  Material Introduction:
    new drill: Follow-the-Leader/safety boat

  Methods/Activities:
    (15 min.) Chalk talk on: a) new water drill Follow-the-Leader that will
          emphasize sail adjustments to the wind, their course, and speed of
          their boats to maintain position in line. Emphasize no contact and
          tiller towards the trouble as a precaution.

    (30 min.) Practice for students as they rig boats.

    (40 min.) Water Drill as students practice Figure-8 Drill. Provide on-the-water
          coaching for sail adjustments and tacking practice.

    (50 min.) Water Drill of students following the safety boat. Safety boat will
          drive in a pattern that causes students to sail from a close reach to a
          broad reach with some tacking. Provide some assistance regarding
          sail adjustments throughout the drill.

    (20 min) Practice for students de-rigging the 420s making sure boats are
          secured and sails/equipment are properly stowed away.

  Closure:
    (20 min.) Review avoiding collisions. Provide some quizzing through
          Questions & Answers on scoop method, parts of boat and sail.
          Provide individual evaluations of strong points and areas for
          improvement.

REMARKS/COMMENTS:
Most of students grasp concepts introduced to date very well. Will be moving on to
upwind sailing.

Sample: Blank Lesson Plan

Lesson Plan for:_____   **Date:**

Lesson Number: _____

Objective/Goal:

Materials:
-                                 -
-                                 -
-                                 -

Content:

    Review: _ -

    Material Introduction:

    Methods/Activities:
        (   )-

        (   )-

        (   )-

        (   )-

    Closure:
        (   )-

.

Remarks/Comments:

Teaching New Skills

For new skills, focus on teaching essential core skills until students are near to mastery before you address lower priority, technical improvements. This is the essence of the building block method of instruction so you, and future instructors, can build upon good, solid skills.

When you are introducing a goal or skill, the design of your lesson must follow a format from which your students will benefit most. **The *cognitive learning method* outlined below represents the progression from a learning phase through the automatic phase to facilitate the learning of new skills.**

Cognitive Learning Method

Step 1 -- Theory Learning Phase. The Theory Learning Phase introduces students to new ideas and concepts which may be totally unfamiliar. The "no-pressure" learning environment of a classroom chalk talk presentation, with appropriate props, diagrams, role playing, and

> **GOAL: Introduction of a new skill** through *classroom chalk talks* with appropriate props, diagrams, role playing and handouts.

handouts will allow your students to formulate a theoretical understanding of the skill or goal you are introducing. Students can focus on learning the theory of a new skill in this secure environment rather than struggle with the complexity of learning the theory and sailing the boat in a water drill at the same time. While students may have a strong theoretical understanding after this first stage of a lesson, they will not yet be able to perform the desired skill. **Instructors should provide an opportunity for students to learn the theoretical aspect of a new skill before sailing.**

Step 2 -- Spatial/Physical Learning Phase. Even though a student may understand the theory of a new skill or topic, there is no reason to believe

> **GOAL: Physical skill development** through *Land Drills*.

that they have developed the physical ability to perform the skill. Sailing skills are often complex and require balance, strength and timing. **Land Drills offer students the opportunity to develop a physical understanding of a new theory they have just learned.** After building student confidence and knowledge through a land drill, you move on to the next step in your lesson where students now go on the water for actual practice of a skill.

Step 3. -- Practical/Consolidation Phase. A Water Drill allows students to merge the smaller segments of a skill (practiced in a land

> **GOAL: Practice of physical skills** through *Water Drills*.

drill) **and incorporate them into a complex skill or activity**. Remember to provide specific supervision until students are comfortable and capable of executing skills in the water drill.

Step 4. -- Automation Phase. An instructor can then increase a student's learning progression from practice to automation through the integration of

> GOAL: Application of skills through the integration of *games*.

games. (See "Games -- Teaching the FUN Way" later in this section.) Water drills can become boring and monotonous for students, but most students will try to expand their abilities and excel in a game. The additional stimuli of water games allows students to master skills due to their instinct to meet the challenge of the game, rather than focusing on the actual desired skill. The net result is that students will challenge themselves and push to excel in a game where they might have become paralyzed through analysis by continuing a water drill.

Learning through Correlational Connections.

When you learn something for the first time, it is difficult to understand the topic without a context or correlational connections. Effective instructors know that their students will struggle with new material until they gain a point of **reference with something they already understand**. For instance, teaching a young student about apparent wind through the technical explanation of vectors and velocity will be fundamentally confusing to most students. Usually, technical terms lose an audience and create confusion in students. Describing apparent wind to students as the breeze they feel when they ride a bicycle or stick their hand out of the window of a moving car is a connection that nearly all students can comprehend. With a proper description and diagram, students will even understand that the velocity at which the bicycle is moving will effect how much apparent wind deviates from actual ("true") wind. It is only when apparent wind is described as a correlation to something that the students already know that they will be able to grasp what would otherwise be a difficult and technical concept.

Whenever instructors introduce a new skill to their students, it is essential that they use a simile to provide their students with a connection to something they already understand. Explaining that the wind that a bike rider feels is "like" the apparent wind generated by the movement of a boat, or that the velocity at which the bike moves is "similar" to a boat's change of velocity efffecting the apparent wind, provides a student with a context for a quick connection to the new material.

When using Correlational Connections there is virtually no subject which is too difficult to teach. Everyone has a bank of information stored in their memory which is used to comprehend new things. This is where the building block method becomes critical to teaching sailors new skills.

The challenge is for the instructor to find a way of making a connection between the new subject matter and something that all their students already understand when introducing each new skill and concept. A solid foundation of understanding allows students to improve at a faster rate and learn skills more rapidly.

Closure and Review

Do not forget to **leave some time at the beginning and end of each lesson to review present and past topics of study, and to provide constructive criticism for each student**. Providing constructive criticism (see *Criticism Sandwich* in Section 1) will allow your students to focus on areas that concern them exclusively and alert them to specific areas where they need to learn or practice for mastery. Also, allowing a few moments at the end of each class to **review the 2-3 central concepts** keeps everyone on the same track.

When you have finished teaching a lesson, take a few moments to **record how the lesson worked**. Did it go as you expected? Would you change anything? Did anything important happen with one of your students? Notes addressing these areas will help you make student evaluations at the end of the course, and allow the program director to make modifications to the course or curriculum.

Land Drills

Major lessons and conceptual material are best taught on land where the teaching environment can be better controlled. On the water, with boats in motion, there is little opportunity for sustained discussion, and there are often too many distractions and impediments to hearing such as luffing sails, wind, and safety boat engine noise. While students may have a strong theoretical understanding of a skill introduced in the classroom, they will not yet be able to perform the desired skill.

The best time to practice a new or complex skill is in a **land drill** before students go sailing. A land drill allows students to physically practice skills and learn drills spatially. *Be sure to explain the concept of a land drill and its purpose.* Providing a land drill will allow you to have a controlled atmosphere in which:

- A complex skill or activity can be broken down into smaller segments and practiced at the desired pace.
- Students can begin to develop a spatial/physical understanding of the skill through simulated practice.
- Students can practice without avoidance behavior or fear.

Making use of the existing elements will heighten the value of a land drill. For example, locate the real wind direction and make sure that a land drill for tacking crosses head-to-wind with the real wind. Supplying additional elements for a land drill, like props or materials that simulate the real situation make a land drill still more effective. "Walking through" a water drill on land, practicing skills on shore that will be required once they are on the water, will help strengthen students' understanding, ability, and confidence once they are sailing.

Make sure that each student takes an active role in your drill and practices the skill. Leaving anyone out of the drill decreases the kinesthetic value of your lesson. *Don't forget that every student must participate in a land drill for it to be effective!* Some ideas for land drills might be, but are not limited to:

- Tacking and Jibing
- Points of sail
- Overboard recovery
- Leaving from and returning to a dock
- Scoop method capsize recovery
- Land sailing
- Trimming a sail relative to the wind (try using a small sail with a mast and boom)
- Pulling the main sheet in properly
- Turning the boat (try using an upside-down picnic table)

TEACHING TIP FOR LAND DRILLS...
A frequently practiced land drill is "tacking." Basic props include two chairs, a tiller with extension, and a line. It is often good to start with a student who "knows everything." Ask him or her to show the class how to tack. Thank and tell the student that he or she did a good job. Then ask the student to explain to the class, exactly how to tack, step by step. Most students usually get it about 50% right. Do the tack with the student one more time, filling in all the details.

Land Drills for Improving Sailing Skills

*Trapping Mainsheet - To transfer mainsheet to the tiller, pass it behind you and firmly grab tiller and mainsheet.

Walking Tacking Drill

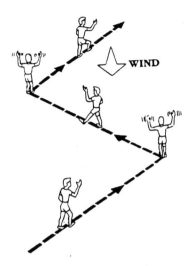

WIND

Tacking Drill (Helmsman)

To practice ashore, three stools, a broom handle and length of rope represent the boat as shown in 1.

1.

Push tiller away from you. Facing forward, step across boat, crouch to avoid boom, shift body to opposite side.

2.

Trapping mainsheet in sheet hand* reach sheet hand behind you to grab tiller.

3.

Sit down on opposite side. Front hand reaches across chest to pick up sheet from tiller hand.

Walking Jibing Drill

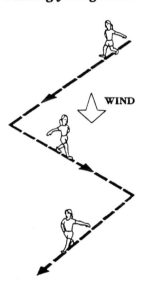

WIND

Jibing Drill (Helmsman)

1.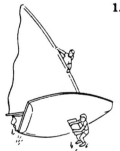

Preparing to Jibe...grab main-sheet parts, pull tiller toward you, step across boat and crouch to avoid boom as you guide it across.

2.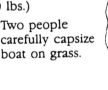

As boat shifts, center yourself and, facing forward, reach sheet arm behind and grasp tiller and sheet — freeing other hand.

3.

Sit down on opposite side. With new front arm, reach across chest to take sheet. Adjust sheet to retain speed on new course.

Right-of-Way Walking Drill

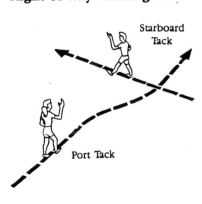

Starboard Tack

Port Tack

Capsize Recovery Land Drill
(for boats under 150 lbs.)

1. Two people carefully capsize boat on grass.

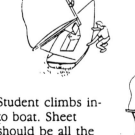

WIND

2. Student leans on daggerboard and starts to re-right boat.

3. Student climbs in-to boat. Sheet should be all the way out with sail luffing.

Water Drills

After building student confidence and knowledge through a land drill, the next step in your lesson plan is to move to the water for actual practice of a skill in the controlled atmosphere of a **water drill**. The water drill allows students to merge the smaller segments of a skill (practiced in the land drill) and incorporate them into the complex skill or activity.

Remember to provide specific supervision until students are comfortable and capable of executing skills in the water drill.

The water drill can also be broken into component parts of the complex composite skill. Beginning students, and students learning complex skills, are best served by breaking a skill into component parts until they gain confidence and approach mastery of each component. On-the-water communication is difficult so all that has been said so far about communication still applies. But now, there are some special considerations.

Predetermined procedures. These include prescribed routines for launching and hauling boats, where the class should gather on the water, what to do in case of a sudden squall or other emergency, etc.

Predetermined procedures create a sense of order and predictability.

For safety reasons all students, instructors, and shore personnel should understand precisely where the class is expected to gather. A fleet which scatters is impossible to communicate with or supervise properly. A suitable prescribed gathering point should be clearly defined or marked with a buoy, so there is no confusion about where to meet.

Every student should be familiar with prescribed emergency procedures, so they know what to do if on-the-water communication becomes difficult or impossible.

Water Drill Preparation. Buoys are essential and can be inexpensive to provide if you use things like hippity hops and blow-up beach toys. The weights can be from weight lifting sets (specifically the cement-filled plastic kind since there are no sharp edges or rust). Before your class begins, set up the water drill course so you don't waste time tossing buoys into the water and arranging them on the fly. This preparation will allow you to make the course "perfect" before everyone gets out to the sailing site, and provide a destination for your students before they leave the dock.

> ☞ **INSTRUCTORS TAKE NOTE...**
> As your students improve their skills and if you are setting a starting line, it is important to have your starting buoys square to the wind and spaced an appropriate distance from each other for the number of boats.

It is also advisable to have a "congregating spot" in close proximity to the launching area for the entire class before heading out to the water drill site as a group. This allows everyone to get rigged and organized for class before moving to the sailing area, and provides warm-up time for tacks or jibes before starting the water drill.

Never leave your students unattended! Accompany them to and from any sailing venue providing general supervision in case they need assistance.

Demonstrations. "Show them what you mean" is a critical element of effective teaching. It sets a visual standard of performance for students to imitate. Students often imitate what they have seen rather than do what they were told. So it is important to conduct all demonstrations properly, "by the book."

Diagram a water drill on shore, and even walk through a land drill simulation of the water drill, before heading out on the water. Do not cut corners or take liberties with standard procedures. It may only instill bad habits you will have to correct later.

Communicating on the Water. There are many impediments to communication when your students are in their boats so review on-the-water procedures and drills before going out to sail.

Once on the water, the communication you can have with individual students will be extremely brief, probably something on the order of 4-10 seconds as they sail along. Frame all feedback in a "criticism sandwich" and deliver the information as quickly and clearly as you can. This will inevitably require that you use "information rich" dialogue.

> **TEACHING TIP FOR WATER DRILLS...**
> • Remember to use direct commands in the early stages of a water drill. Indirect commands can be used to prompt students after they have learned, but not mastered, a skill.
> • When you communicate with students on the water, make sure you are upwind of the students so the wind will help carry your message.

To convey rich precise information, *prioritize* the things that each student needs to improve upon. Communicate how they can improve one or two items highest on the priority list, like a hand pass during a tack, sitting in the correct position, or holding the tiller correctly, as they are some of the core areas of improvement.

Don't overload a student with multiple areas of improvement because they will only be able to process one or two suggestions at a time. Reserve some structured time after sailing for an overall summary and more detailed commentary.

Laying Out Courses for Water Drills. In general, compact sailing drill courses, whose turning marks are no more than 2 to 4 minutes sailing time apart, are more motivating for students than longer courses. Short courses:

- Provide instructors with better group control.
- Provide opportunities for more frequent positive reinforcement by allowing the students to reach each destination more often in the available time.
- Provide more practice in turning maneuvers. Repetition is an important ingredient in learning.
- Concentrate boats into a smaller area. Close proximity allows better communication from a safety boat as well as better visual comparison between boats. In close quarters students silently learn from one another by watching and comparing results.

When teaching first-time beginners, set your course well upwind of a lee shore or other downwind obstruction. You can expect frequent steering errors from new helmsmen and occasional time spent drifting in irons. Because of these understandable mishaps, beginners often wander farther downwind than you had intended. Taking precautions in the way you lay out a course can help to avoid such troubles and keep your lesson fun and productive.

When devising a course configuration, tailor it to the overall lesson plan of the day. Select the more controlled drills in the beginning (like the Crosswind Figure-8 Drill) and then move to the more complex ones (like Tacking on the Whistle) This allows students to consolidate skills and achieve some level of success before moving on. Another example would be, if you want to work on jibes, rather than using a single-jibe triangle, consider a windward-leeward course with a slalom leeward leg. It makes more constructive use of the available time, because it provides more practice jibes following each trip upwind.

Station your safety boat at a mark so you can give feedback to each student. Remember to vary the direction students go around the buoys while doing the drills so they aren't always doing port roundings. Some of the things to look for in a drill like the Crosswind Figure-8 Drill are:

> Tacking facing forward
> Body placement and fore and aft trim
> Sitting opposite sail
> Tiller hand exchange
> Sheeting in as the boat heads up
> Sheeting out as the boat bears off

Remember that your students are somewhat like a school of fish. If you can get a few to start a water drill, the rest should follow. Also your safety boat will hopefully work like a magnet so you can often lead them into a drill.

Water Drills for Improving Sailing Skills

Stop and Start Solo Drill

Safety Position Solo Drill

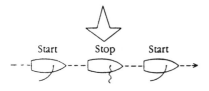

Circling Solo Drill

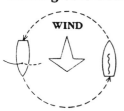

Glide Zone Solo Drill

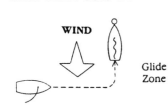

Leaving and Returning Drill

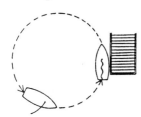

Man-Overboard (MOB) Drill

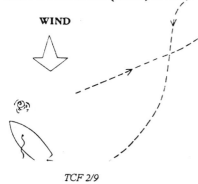

Oval Upwind - Downwind Drill

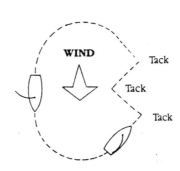

Oval Tacking & Jibing Drill

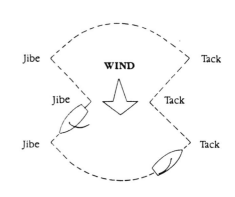

Group Practice

Stop and Start Group Drill

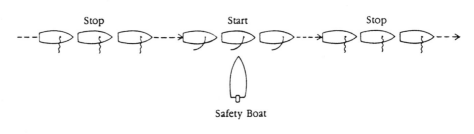

Safety Position Group Drill

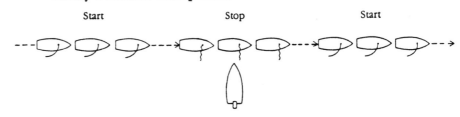

Follow-the-Leader Drill

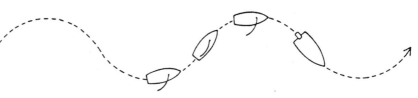

Crosswind Figure-8 Drill

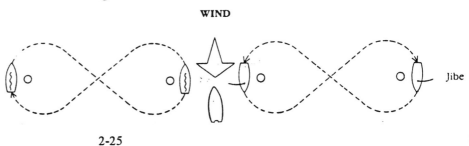

Group Drills continued

Circle Safety Boat Drill

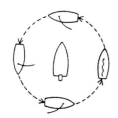

Crosswind Loop Drill

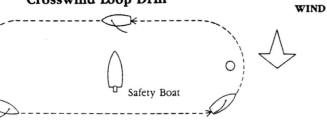

Safety Boat

WIND

Oval Upwind - Downwind Drill

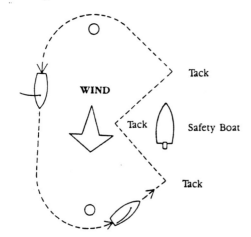

WIND

Tack

Tack

Safety Boat

Tack

Oval Tacking - Jibing Drill

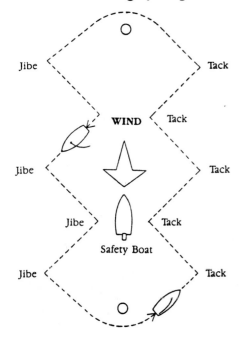

Jibe

Jibe

Jibe

Jibe

Jibe

WIND

Tack

Tack

Tack

Tack

Tack

Safety Boat

Rectangular Course Drill

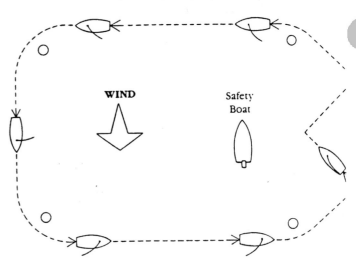

WIND

Safety Boat

Leaving and Returning Drill

WIND

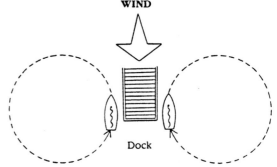

Dock

Coming Alongside Drill

WIND

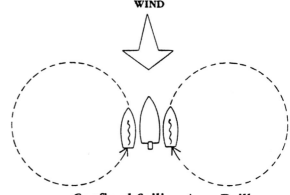

Confined Sailing Area Drill

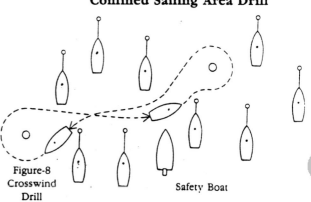

Figure-8
Crosswind
Drill

Safety Boat

Games -- Teaching the FUN Way

A good instructor can increase a student's learning progression from practice to automation through the integration of games. As drills become repetitive, the need for practice may still exist, but students begin to experience boredom. The additional stimuli of games allows students to master skills due to their instinct to meet the challenge of the game, rather than focusing on the actual desired skill. Under the guise of games, they can continue to practice without recognizing the old repetitive drills. Their primary focus becomes fun and enjoyment rather than concentrating on skills and development. However, **turning drills into games can easily become self-defeating if they create performance anxiety. THE DESIGN OF GAMES SHOULD BE COMPATIBLE WITH A STUDENT'S ABILITY LEVEL** and should avoid situations where an individual is compared to other students.

GAME POSSIBILITIES			
TEAM GAMES		INDIVIDUAL GAMES	
Team vs. Itself	[Lowest Anxiety]	Individual vs. Him/Herself	
Team vs. Performance		Individual vs. Performance	
Team vs. Time		Individual vs. Time	
Team vs. Team	[Highest Anxiety]	Individual vs. Individual	

Naturally, the game's design should incorporate the skills being practiced. Map out the game you intend to play before beginning any drills so the overall lesson will follow a more logical progression. You may use land drills as a method of introducing and demonstrating your on-the-water games, or you can have games on land that reinforce sailing knowledge. This will provide sailing students with a fun and entertaining forum, maximizing class time and learning through lesson continuity. US SAILING's publication, *Teach Sailing the Fun Way,* **is a good resource for creative activities as well as the "Creative Activities for Sailing Programs" Appendix in the** *Small Boat Sailing Level 1 Instructor Manual.*

Key ingredients to "teach the FUN way" include:
- **Present standard material in creative ways --** that rabbit has been coming out of the hole forever! Why not try a new story?
- **Try for 100% group participation.**
- **Remember Safety, Fun and Learning.**
- **Provide variety.**
- **Be prepared --** organize materials that you need ahead of time.
- **Brainstorm with other instructors.**
- **Get involved --** the more excited you are, the more fun it will be for the whole group. Remember, you are a role model; and if you are enthusiastic about the activity, your group will be too.
- **Seize the teachable moment -- learning is what is fun!**

Final Thoughts On Curriculum Planning

When developing or revising a curriculum, it is helpful to get feedback from the students and instructors who were involved in the last course. **To help with future planning, the program director should prepare weekly reports describing how instructors have actually spent their time in comparison to the program plan.** To further aid assessment of the program, instructor's notations on each lesson plan allow insight into the merits and weaknesses of a plan. Record keeping in these areas will help in making adjustments to the curriculum.

Parents In a Junior Sailing Program

One of the biggest questions program organizers and instructors have to address is the degree of parent involvement in a sailing program. Sailing is a participation sport. Unlike spectator sports, such as football and baseball, provisions for spectators in sailing events is difficult.

Setting a policy

Program organizers should develop a policy that permits sailing instructors to teach without outside interference. This involves establishment of an integrated program which includes parent in specific activities and yet restricts parents from the instructional area.

Some parents may not be happy with such an arrangements. These parents should be reminded that they would not barge into a schoolroom to take the teacher to task, not would they enter the operating room to tell the physician what to do. Explain that sailing instructors are employees who have a right to a proper work environment and a responsibility to all of their students. To mitigate parental concerns about the direction of instruction, give them a voice in the off season. Parental input to the design and development of the entire program can improve the overall program immensely. Finally, the program organizers and instructors must strongly enforce this policy and not tolerate any disruption of the sailing program. Any questions regarding the sailing program can be directed to the Head Instructor or Program Organizers during posted office hours.

Parent Orientation Sessions

It is essential that at some prior stage to the start of the program, program organizers should call a parent orientation session to explain the details of the program. Included in this orientation should be a review of how parents can be involved in the program (parent day, guest speaker, car pools, chaperones, race committee, social activity organizers), the rules for the program, and the disciplinary code. Program organizers and instructors should be frank with parents about their intention to maintain the integrity of a program by dismissing persistent offenders.

The orientation should detail student drop-off and pick-up arrangements, emphasizing that students must be prompt for class and must be picked up at the correct time. Instructors must not be expected to baby-sit class members who are waiting to be picked up.

The professional nature of the program should be stressed, along with the planning that has gone into its development. Organizers should detail the training that instructors have undergone and the usefulness the training will provide in relation to the students, organization, and parents. Parents should be reminded that continued cooperation and support will further the sailing program's success.

Parent Participation and Information Updating

Set up opportunities throughout the program for parents to participate. These opportunities can include cookouts, displays, and open day. A mid-season newsletter, written by the students, can provide more information to the parents on program events. Planned events like these are essential to retain the interest of the parents and also provide the instructors an opportunity to discuss the progress of each student.

For programs running on a shoestring budget with volunteer instructors, it is especially important to discuss the role of parents can play in the program's success, either as helpers or fund raisers.

Involvement of Parents and Students in Program Planning

Regular meetings with parents helps to get them working for you and with you. These meetings provide a forum for discussing the sailing program. Ask for the parent's input on the program and any related topics at the end of the season, and invite them to evaluate and improve the program in the off season.

About four to six weeks after the end of the training program, organize a social event for the students. Organize a social event, or show sailing films of the previous season's activities.

Set time aside to ask each of the classes what they liked and disliked about their courses. Collate this information so you can discuss it at the next program organizers' meeting. The program organizers will use this information to prepare a comprehensive program outline (curriculum) for the upcoming season. Once the program organizers have received the students' and parents' input on the program, program planning can be finalized. Program planning should be developed early so proper instructor job descriptions can be prepared to hire the instructional staff next season.

Several weeks before a program starts, all information relating to the upcoming sailing program should be sent out to participants. This is also the time when enrollment takes place. Rather than having parents main in applications, checks, and indemnity forms, change the registration format so that enrollment is through personal appearance with the students present. This method ensures that both the parents and students understand the nature of the course, including equipment, safety, and swimming ability, etc. The enrollment day should coincide with a function at the program facility to encourage turnout. If this isn't possible, enrollment should be held during a weekend with the sessions at 9 a.m., 1 p.m., and 3 p.m., to ensure that all parents can attend with their children. Show films and serve refreshments to capture the interest of the participants and establish enthusiasm early in the season. Parents should bring all necessary medical documents, disclaimers, consent forms, as a condition of enrollment.

Just prior to the start of the sailing program, a social evening for students and parents should be held as an ideal method to introduce the sailing instructors. Go over the main points of the program, including any new classes or activities.

Teaching Children vs. Teaching Adults

Children and adults have a number of different learning requirements which an instructor should take into account:

1. Kids have shorter attention spans than adults. Keep their classroom sessions brief and well focused. You may not have long to get your point across before you lose them.

2. Both children and adults need structure in their learning environment, but kids need it more. Adults are usually more self-disciplined about staying focused in seeking a goal. Kids live more for the moment.

3. Kids need concrete examples, specific instructions and clear objectives. Adults appreciate analogies and are better equipped to handle abstractions and applying theory to practice.

4. Everyone's motives are different. Younger kids seek approval, acceptance and fun; while adults value social interaction and a sense of progress.

5. Adults benefit from reflection time. Kids benefit more from repetition.

6. Kids enjoy and get more out of learning in groups than in private lessons.

Teaching Girls and Women

Children's sailing programs usually start out with roughly equal numbers of boys and girls. But as they grow older, more girls drop out than boys. As young children, boys and girls are about the same size and their differences are less pronounced. As they develop physically, boys generally grow larger and develop more upper body strength. Their extra weight hiking out helps with heel control, and their upper body strength makes many routine chores such as mainsail trimming easier. To keep girls from becoming discouraged and dropping out,try the following.

1. Have female instructors on staff to serve as role models. They are more likely to appreciate the interests and concerns of female students.

2. Use sailboats suitable for the weight and strength of the program's female participants. In a race a 110 pound 14 year old girl is at a distinct disadvantage against a 150 pound 14 year old boy in many singlehanded boats, especially in stronger winds. A doublehanded boat or a smaller boat with less sail area helps even the score.

3. Special girls' or women's sailing classes or clinics can help boost camaraderie and enthusiasm. In racing programs, competition can be divided into weight classes.

4. Be on guard to spot any fear producing or intimidating situations. Younger girls may not feel comfortable sailing doublehanded with aggressively competitive boys or much older girls.

5. Foster a comfortable atmosphere of sportsmanship and cooperation. If the boys and girls both feel comfortable and have fun, they're likely to stay with the program.

FORM 1 -- FACILITY INSPECTION
GUIDELINES

PREMISES

1. Are exterior premises, including driveways, walkways, parking areas, ramps, docks, etc. in safe condition?

2. Are launch ramps of solid construction, offering good traction and adequate room for maneuvering?

3. Are the launching and staging areas free of overhead power line hazards?

4. Is a power hoist in use?

5. Is its operation restricted to staff?

6. Is the insured responsible for any piers, docks, or moorings?

7. Is so, are these properly arranged and maintained?

8. If located in tidal waters, is the design appropriate for changing water levels?

9. Is the space for sailing class well lighted and ventilated?

10. Is there a telephone and/or some means of contacting emergency help, if needed?

HOUSEKEEPING

1. Are facilities clean and well kept?

2. Is there proper trash storage and trash removal?

3. Are boats and equipment stored safely to prevent falling, vandalism, or theft and with adequate passageways for the equipment used to remove boats?

MAINTENANCE

1. Are facilities and equipment well maintained?

2. Is preventive maintenance done on a written schedule?

3. Are mechanical systems maintained by qualified persons?

SAFETY

1. Is an Emergency Action Plan posted?

2. Is there a First Aid kit available? If it is stored in a locked place, where is the key kept?

3. Is fire protection equipment provided?

4. Indicate which equipment is available:

   ☐ Sprinklers
   ☐ Extinguishers
   ☐ Smoke or Heat Detection
   ☐ Standpipe/Hose
   ☐ Fire Alarm

5. Do the safety boat(s) have radios and required safety equipment? If it is not on the boat(s), where is it stored? If it is stored in a locked place, where is the key kept?

6. Is there a procedure for record keeping and inspections?

FORM 2 -- MEDICAL &
EMERGENCY INFORMATION

(This form must be completed and signed by you or your parents (if you are a minor) and turned in prior to the start of your course.)

Name _____ Birth date _____ Sex _____

Address _____
No.   Street   City   State   Zip

Do you have a history of, or do you currently have, any physical limitations that might prevent you from fully participating in this course? _____ Yes _____ No   If yes, please specify missing or injured bodily parts, weakness, eyeglasses, contacts, hearing aids, etc. _____
_____

Do you have any learning disability that might prevent you from fully participating in this course? _____ Yes _____ No   If yes, please specify _____

Please check ( ) those that apply and provide necessary information on reverse side of this form.

Chronic Ailments:
    Asthma, or other respiratory problems _____
    Circulatory or heart problems _____
    Diabetes or hypoglycemia _____
    Epilepsy _____
    Hemophilia, or other bleeding problems _____

Allergies:
    Insect bites _____
    Bee stings _____
    Foods _____
    Drugs _____
    Others, if significant _____

Current medications or pertinent information _____

Blood type _____   Date of last tetanus shot _____

Family physician name _____   Phone _____

Date of most recent physical examination _____

Where are your medical records kept? _____

Insurance Carrier _____   Insurance ID # _____

Who should be notified in case of emergency?

Name _____ Relation _____

Phone _____ (B) _____ (R)

Name _____ Relation _____

Phone _____ (B) _____ (R)

I, the undersigned, do hereby authorize and consent to any x-ray examination, anesthetic, medical or surgical diagnosis or procedure rendered under the general or specific supervision of any member of the medical staff or of a dentist licensed under the provisions of the Education Law and/or Public Health Law of the State of _____ and on the staff of any hospital holding a current operating certificate issued by the Department of Health of the State of _____. It is understood that this authorization is given in advance of any specific diagnosis, treatment or hospital care being required but is given to provide authority and power to render care which the aforementioned physician in the exercise of his/her best judgment may deem advisable. It is understood that effort shall be made to contact the above people prior to rendering treatment to the patient, but that any of the above treatment will not be withheld if any of these people cannot be reached.

Signature _____ Date _____
          Applicant, or Parent/Guardian (if a minor)

FORM 3 -- EMERGENCY PROCEDURE

In the event of an emergency or incident, the *DUTY MANAGER* will:

1. **GET HELP...**

   FIRE:
   - Get people and staff out of the area
   - Call <u>911</u>

   INJURY:
   - Provide immediate first aid
   - Call <u>911</u>
   - Disburse onlookers

   INCIDENT:
   Robbery, obnoxious customer, collision (boat/car), trespasser, stolen property/boat
   - Call <u>Police at</u> _____

   For less serious incidents (i.e., Coast Guard/Harbor Police stop, private boat unaccounted for, etc.)
   - Contact <u>Marina Supervisor</u> _____

   LOST RENTAL BOAT:
   - Make sure all boats are accounted for at closing time.
   - Search for boats before dark (all boats should be in sight one hour before closing) and take a VHF radio
   - Have the office attendant monitor channel 68
   - If boat cannot be found, call <u>Harbor Police at</u> _____

2. **THEN CALL...**   Manager _____
                             Assistant Manager   _____
                             Office Supervisor   _____

3. **The above will contact** or (if the Duty Manager is unable to reach one of the above supervisors) the *DUTY MANAGER* will report to:
                             Assistant Director   _____
                             Director   _____
                             Owner   _____

4. **The Owner is to be notified** at _____ in the event of fire, serious injuries, and incidents requiring assistance from other law enforcement or emergency response agencies.

5. **Accidents, injuries, and incidents MUST be reported** in writing as soon as possible after their occurrence to the Marina Manager. Reports will be submitted no later than the end of the shift following the incident.

FORM 4 -- PARTICIPATION AGREEMENT

The Basic Sailing course you are about to begin is an exciting and demanding challenge, but you need to be aware of what will be involved and be willing to study and practice to achieve success.

A swim test is required of all students, which consists of swimming 50 yards in the waters of the area you will be sailing in, in sailing clothing and footwear. The attached student registration and medical and emergency information form must be completed and signed by you or your parents (if you are a minor) and turned in no later than _____.

You will be required to provide a life jacket (vest type) which should be Coast Guard approved, the proper size for your weight and build, and be form fitting and comfortable, as you will be wearing it at all times during the course. Put your name on it with waterproof ink. Proper footwear will also be worn at all times, both on land and on the water. Bring a change of clothes, a towel, a lined notebook for note taking, two pencils, and a waterproof felt tip pen to each lesson.

The fee for this course is _____.   Your instructor will be _____.
Lessons begin on _____, starting at _____ AM / PM and ending at _____ AM / PM.

I understand that in entering this sailing course I agree to obey all program rules as set forth by the program director and the instructors, that I will use utmost care in the use of the boats and equipment, that I will not engage in any horseplay or other disruptive behavior. I understand that failure to attend regularly, arrive promptly, abide by the rules may result in my suspension from the program.

Applicant's Signature _____   Date _____

I assume full responsibility for any loss or damage, excepting loss or damage covered by insurance, that may come to any person, boat, sailboard, equipment, pier, float, or other property used in conjunction with this course as the result of improper use, negligence, violation of the rules, and other acts of sailors, or other representatives of the school, instructional program or host location in connection herewith. I accept that the sport of sailing and the conduct of this course entail and are subject to certain inherent risks and assume all risks on land and on the water of participation in this program. I further agree to hold the school, instructional program or host location, US SAILING, and their representatives harmless for personal injuries and/or property damage.

Signature _____   Date _____
                Applicant, or Parent/Guardian (if a minor)

Parental/Guardian Agreement (if student is a minor):

I understand the contents of this statement and agree to see to it that my child adheres to the program rules. I agree to assume the obligation for the expenses of repair and/or replacement of program equipment that is attributable to my child's reckless or irresponsible behavior. I agree to make an appointment for a parent-instructor conference if requested.

Parent/Guardian's Signature _____   Date _____

FORM 5 -- INJURY REPORT

INJURED:

Person _____ Age ____ Sex ____

Address _____
         No.   Street   City   State   Zip

Phone _____ (B) _____ (R)

Association with program _____

INJURY:

Describe injury _____

Where taken _____

Name of Physician/Hospital _____

Physician's diagnosis _____

First Aid administered by _____

Time First Aid administered _____ AM / PM

ACCIDENT:

Date _____ Time _____ AM / PM

Address _____
         No.   Street   City   State   Zip

Exact location at address _____

Describe accident _____

_____

Names, addresses, and telephone numbers of witnesses:

1. _____

2. _____

3. _____

List below: weather conditions; water conditions; water temperature; air temperature; tide conditions; boat and equipment particulars.

Draw diagram below if a collision was involved.

Report prepared by _____ Date _____

Signature _____

Reviewed by _____ Date _____

Signature _____

Corrective measures _____

Date person returned to program _____

Restrictions on activities _____

FORM 6 -- STUDENT REGISTRATION

FEE PAID _____

DATE _____

Applicant (applicant to complete):

Name _____ Birth date _____ Sex _____

Address _____
No.　　Street　　　　　　　City　　　　　　　State　　Zip

Phone _____ (B) _____ (R)

- -

Parent/Guardian (parent/guardian to complete if applicant is a minor):

Father's name _____

Phone _____ (B) _____ (R)

Mother's name _____

Phone _____ (B) _____ (R)

Emergency contact _____
　　　　　　　　　Name　　　　　　　　　Phone　　　　　Relation

Signature _____ Date _____

- -

Course Information (applicant to complete):

Can you swim approximately 50 yards, using
any stroke, in sailing clothing and shoes/booties? _____ Yes _____ No _____ Not sure

Will you be available for all lessons? _____ Yes _____ No

If not, are you prepared to take a make-up lesson? _____ Yes _____ No

Your previous sailing experience _____

What personal goals do you hope to achieve by taking this course? _____

_____

I assume full responsibility for any loss or damage, excepting loss or damage covered by insurance, that may come to any person, boat, sailboard, equipment, pier, float, or other property used in conjunction with this course as the result of improper use, negligence, violation of the rules, and other acts of sailors, or other representatives of the school, instructional program or host location in connection herewith. I accept that the sport of sailing and the conduct of this course entail and are subject to certain inherent risks and assume all risks on land and on the water of participation in this program. I further agree to hold the school, instructional program or host location, US SAILING, and their representatives harmless for personal injuries and/or property damage.

Signature _____   Date _____
           Applicant, or Parent/Guardian (if a minor)

- -

Instructor Record (instructor to complete):

SWIM TEST PASSED _____ Yes _____ No   Date _____

COURSE COMPLETED _____ Yes _____ No   Date _____

Signature _____   Date _____

- -

POLICY GUIDELINES

As a sailing instructor or administrator of a program it is important to develop site-specific policies which will handle day to day administration needs and emergency situations. Listed below are some subjects that should be considered if teaching or administering a sailing program.

- Emergency Procedures for:
  - ☑ Injury
  - ☑ Overboard Recovery
    - ✓ Sailboat recovery
    - ✓ Powerboat recovery
  - ☑ Vessel collision with possibility of sinking
  - ☑ Grounding
  - ☑ Fire (afloat and ashore)
  - ☑ Weather change (squall or thunderstorm)
- Record Keeping Procedures
- Student Discipline
- Student Dissatisfaction
- Broken Equipment
- Radio Use
- Life Jacket (PFD) Use
- Non-Emergency Medical Transportation or Admission
- Non-Injury Vessel Collision and Property Damage
- Employee Personal Equipment Use
- Launching/Hoist Usage
- Insurance
  - ☑ Property
  - ☑ Medical

RECORD KEEPING GUIDELINES

Instructors and administrators have a responsibility to keep accurate written records. A thorough program should include the following.

- Medical Forms
- Permission/Waivers
- Participation Agreements
- Registration Forms
- Swim Test Records
- Attendance Records
- Daily Log
  - ✓ Weather
  - ✓ Unusual Items
- Lesson Plans
- Program Schedules
- Student Lists
- Student Certification Awards
- Course Evaluations
- Equipment List/Inventories
- Equipment Order Forms
- Broken Equipment Forms
- Accident Report Forms
- Job Descriptions
- Employee Discipline
- Time Sheets
- Mailing Lists
- Publicity/Marketing Forms

SECTION 3

TEACHING SAILORS WITH SPECIAL NEEDS

TEACHING SAILORS WITH PHYSICAL DISABILITIES

Teaching from the Heart and Mind

One of the most noble, challenging, and rewarding experiences you may have as a sailing instructor is to teach students with disabilities. As sailing instructors we find many extrinsic rewards. However, *the greatest reward that we all take from our job is the development and growth of our students.* Watching the progress of our pupils from day to day, all the way through to year after year is the single most rewarding aspect of sailing instruction. By **identifying proper goals, and developing lessons to achieve those goals**, an instructor can assist students in achieving and excelling in areas thought unattainable.

Imagine teaching a visually impaired sailor to detect, react and adjust to windshifts, or assisting a paralytic student to gain self-sufficiency in the boat. Perhaps your work as an instructor can aid students with learning disabilities, from Dyslexia to Attention Deficit Disorders, to develop coping mechanisms through their sailing which they can then apply to their lives ashore. The only boundaries to which a good sailing instructor adheres are SAFETY, FUN and LEARNING.

Often, the greatest concern for sailing instructors is getting started. Questions like, "How should I design my classes?", "Do I have to teach differently?" and "Where should I begin?" are all solved with one answer. ***Design and teach classes the same way you would in any setting -- BUT ALSO be sensitive to the students' needs!*** Special consideration may be necessary for such things as: braces and prosthetic devices, the dexterity of students, medications, loss of control or epilepsy, sanitation and bathrooms, etc.; BUT THE FUNDAMENTALS OF TEACHING SAILING still apply.

- **Assess your students' ability levels.**
  When instructing students with physical disabilities or learning disabilities, you must assess not only what their sailing abilities are but also where their disabilities might prove harmful during instructional or sailing situations. You must also know your students' abilities for you to teach at the proper pace and ability level.

- **Understand your students' learning styles.**
  In any teaching situation, you will be most effective when you can teach to the predominant learning styles of your students.

- **Set goals with your students, not for your students.**
  Whenever you set goals, it helps to identify easily attained short term confidence building goals as well as more complex long term goals. A building block approach facilitates this type of student growth.

- **Set class size limits to reflect the desired teacher-to-student ratio.**
  When teaching disabled students who will progress at notably different speeds, it is essential to keep the teacher-to-student ratio very low to provide the necessary individualized attention. The more individualized attention a student requires, the fewer students you should have in the class competing for the instructor's attention.

Your efforts to ensure that classes for disabled students are safe and effective will require **more thorough planning**. You must also educate yourself as much as possible about your students' disabilities so that you can better understand how to help them through the rigors of sailing instruction. While explaining and describing all the possible situations a sailing instructor may have to solve is impossible, the following will help you to make initial decisions, develop a framework of instruction, and introduce you to core strategies and concepts for teaching.

Assessing Physical Disabilities and Essential Functions

In July, 1990, the *Americans with Disabilities Act* (ADA) was signed into law prohibiting discrimination based on disabilities. The ADA requires all affected entities to provide **"reasonable accommodation"** for persons with disabilities. In short, this means that sporting programs must provide opportunities for participation in activities to qualified individuals. Developing a method for reasonable accommodation requires that you know what is required of a "qualified" individual, and what can be considered a "reasonable" accommodation.

To begin, you must make some key assessments of:

- your **facilities and equipment,**
- your **students' functional abilities** which must be jointly determined with your students (and their parents/legal guardian(s) if applicable), and
- the **essential functions required to actively participate in sailing.**

> **AN IMPORTANT ESSENTIAL FUNCTION...**
> Don't forget that swimming and comfort in the water are required for all students!

Pause for a moment to consider what essential functions (such as pulling/pushing, paddling,...) there are in the sport of sailing.

Depending on equipment availability and instructor assistance, **there are few functions that could prevent a disabled student from participating in sailing**. Even communication barriers, one of the most critical functional areas on the water, can usually be overcome with some slight training and accommodation. Your sailing program directors and

> ✓ **ASSESSMENT TIP...**
> Concise definitions of essential functions for sailing will help students assess their abilities when you meet to determine whether they have adequate functionality.

instructors should create a detailed list of the essential functions for sailing. Make sure that you can communicate and defend your definitions. Finally, you should assess whether participation is affected if one essential skill cannot be performed. For instance, if a student cannot swim, and does not feel comfortable in the water, will your sailing program or class be able to develop a reasonable accommodation for that student?

Adequate Functionality

The next step is for the student and instructor/program directors to determine whether a disability will affect performance and require reasonable accommodation. This determination should *never* be made without a consultation with the student. **Students should be asked whether they can perform functions or describe the accommodation they would require.** Students with physical disabilities will require substantially different accommodations and attention. Your program must address issues of accessibility to your facility, docks, boats and equipment in determining reasonable accommodations. The final decision for participation should be determined by whether or not your program can provide reasonable and adequate accommodations for a student. Discuss with the student if they think they are functionally accommodated by the proposals you are able to devise.

Access to the Program

Although the ADA is the law of the land, there are still many facilities which are inadequately prepared for accessibility. For example, in areas where there is a significant tidal shift, steep ramp inclines are a hazard to everyone. Other concerns include the width, freeboard, and stability of floating docks and finger piers. Is there ample and appropriate parking? If you can't get your student safely to the boats, you can't teach them to sail.

Independent Transfer

As you can understand, safely boarding vessels can be tricky and possibly injurious for both the student and the instructor. Some students are extremely independent and may want to transfer themselves into the boat. While this is a desirable goal, as the instructor it's your responsibility to be sure the transfer is conducted safely.

- ☐ Does the student have an **adequate PFD**?
- ☐ **Has the student ever transferred before?**
- ☐ Does the student require **special attention** to get into a boat?
- ☐ Does the student have **sufficient strength for an independent transfer** into a boat?
- ☐ Can the **boat be firmly attached to the dock**? Increased stability is often obtained by letting the bowline out and bringing the stern in close to the dock, then resnugging the bowline.
- ☐ If the transfer is to the dock, are there **splinters**? If so, what can be done to protect the student?

Assisted Carries

If a student does not have the physical strength or the confidence to try an independent transfer, **assisted carries are an option** for transferring a student into the boat. Be sure to ask the student if a carry is acceptable to him/her. Often, a student will have a preferred method which will keep him/her most comfortable. Some factors to consider when effecting a carry include:

> Remember, always ask your students if they would like your assistance **before** you assist them!

- ☐ **Have a plan** as to how you will conduct a carry. **Practice** before attempting an actual carry. You may be surprised by the unforeseen complications involved!
- ☐ Determine how the student is to be picked up (hands/wrist/legs, cross-chest/armpits/legs, support legs, etc.).
- ☐ **Discuss all details of the carry with the student.**
- ☐ Have **spotters** positioned in case lifter(s) lose their balance.
- ☐ Use **cushions** to prevent injury on the dock.
- ☐ **Have the student give the "ready, set, go!"**
- ☐ Always bend at the knees, using your **legs to lift** and keeping your back straight!

Prevention of Sailing Related Injuries

In addition to wanting sailing facilities that are accessible and safe, all students have some concerns about sustaining injuries while involved in physical activities. Students with a lack of sensation can be injured or receive pressure sores without their knowledge.

Proper Facilities

By following some basic preventive measures, you can provide a safer environment for all students:

- ☑ **Pad all exposed sharp or abrasive areas.**
- ☑ **Provide a stable area** in the boat for those students concerned with losing their balance.
- ☑ **Keep lines** running into the cockpit area **tangle free** and as uncluttered as possible.
- ☑ **Acquaint students with the operation of equipment on the boat that could cause injury**, such as blocks, clamps and the boom.
- ☑ **Discuss the boathandling characteristics** of the sailboat you will be using so there are no surprises. Discuss the stability of the boat, its seating, lines and what happens during maneuvers like tacks and jibes in various wind conditions.

Proper Clothing

The old adage, "It's easier to take off something you don't need, than to put on something you didn't take," is perhaps the best advice in preparing to go sailing. Layering is the proven method of dealing with temperature changes. **Some individuals are unable to naturally retain heat or perspire; others may not be able to feel when they are getting too hot or too cold**. As their instructor you will be responsible for helping your students to remain safe and comfortable and provide adequate assistance.

> **A CAUTIONARY NOTE...**
> Temperature related emergencies progress rapidly for some students with physical or developmental disabilities.

Symptoms for heat related emergencies are the same for people with disabilities. However, the onset of an emergency may come more quickly for a sailor with disabilities. Prevention of heat emergencies is the same, though. Drinking plenty of liquids (water is best), having a spray bottle at hand, and keeping skin protected from the elements and the direct effects of the sun will combat injuries.

Poor circulation and lack of muscle movement can rapidly bring on a case of hypothermia. As with any student, the instructor should take preventive measures prior to the student taking to the water. Always be prepared for temperature changes.

Personal Flotation Devices (PFDs)

US SAILING requires all candidates taking a US SAILING Instructor Course to wear PFDs whenever they are *near or on* the water. This policy is highly recommended for *all* students at *all* other times, and it is a good idea to enforce this safety rule regardless of the students' swimming ability. Now is the time to establish safety habits that last a lifetime!

Proper type and fit of the PFD are the responsibility of the instructor. If your program or the student provides the PFD, test fit the PFD under controlled conditions (in a pool for instance) prior to the start of instruction. For individuals with mobility limitations Type I or Type II PFDs provide the greatest degree of flotation.

Capsize Recoveries

Capsize recovery is an essential skill taught to *all* students. When introducing any student to why capsizes happen, explain that this is normal in certain types of sailboats, and then explain how to properly right the boat. Since you've already determined the students' comfort level in the water, taking the next step to capsize recovery should be relatively easy.

Again, patience is a major factor. Some physically stronger students will quickly right the boat (within 1 to 2 minutes), while others require more time (students with weak upper body strength can take as long as 35 minutes) to complete the exercise. **Give students adequate time to figure out a method that works for them, but be on guard against hypothermia.** Not everyone will be able to execute a scoop recovery.

> **A SAFETY POLICY...**
> If a student cannot right a capsizeable boat independently, he or she should not sail solo until a method of capsize recovery is mastered.

Risk Management, Liability and Safety

Section 4 in this manual covers the subject of risk management and liability. As the instructor, **it's your responsibility to clearly explain the risks involved in sailing to all your students (and parents/guardians when applicable).** By getting everyone's concerns into the open, and understanding the inherent dangers in sailing, a final decision about participation can be agreed upon. Once informed of potential risks, it's the student's right (with parental/guardian consent when applicable) to continue with the course of instruction. This mutual understanding of the risks and steps necessary to reduce risks will go a long way toward insuring a safe and enjoyable experience for everyone.

Safe practice and teaching methods are the foundation of US SAILING program of instruction. This does not change when teaching individuals with disabilities.

TEACHING SAILORS WITH LEARNING DISABILITIES

Teaching from the Heart and Mind

People have strengths and weaknesses in terms of how they learn. Students who are diagnosed with Attention Deficit Disorder (ADD), Attention Deficit Hyperactivity Disorder (ADHD), Language Processing or Central Auditory Processing (CAP) problems, and/or Dyslexia generally experience more difficulty learning than other students. If you have ever been in a situation where you "spaced out," couldn't understand verbal directions or struggled with a written passage, you have experienced what learning disabled individuals cope with every day. You can control when you daydream while a person with ADD or ADHD has much more difficulty remaining focused. For you processing information, reading and writing do not require the extra time and effort that a learning disabled student needs to comprehend information and complete tasks.

Characteristics of learning disabilities may include some of the following, but are not limited to:

- ☐ Short attention span
- ☐ Restlessness
- ☐ Impulsiveness
- ☐ Organizational difficulty
- ☐ Difficulty reading or comprehending written materials
- ☐ Difficulty understanding and following verbal directions and information
- ☐ Difficulty starting and finishing projects
- ☐ Relational difficulty
- ☐ Spatial difficulty
- ☐ Easily-triggered anger
- ☐ Negative internal feelings and self-image
- ☐ Low energy
- ☐ Normal IQ
- ☐ Very messy handwriting

While some learning disability characteristics can be treated with medication, you, as an instructor, must also take measures to accommodate students with learning disabilities. If students exhibit several of these symptoms, you may want to contact their parents/guardians for some suggestions on teaching and behavior management techniques.

Class size, structure, rules, plans and activities must all be adjusted to accommodate students with learning disabilities. In many cases, students with learning disabilities will not require substantial accommodations because they have been able to develop coping mechanisms which allow them to function at a higher level.

Due to the nature of learning disability characteristics, an instructor's teaching style must take into consideration the learning needs of his or her students. Review the list of symptoms mentioned earlier. What alterations would you make to accommodate a student with learning disabilities?

> ✎ **INSTRUCTORS TAKE NOTE...**
> Often, people will hesitate to inform you of a disability to avoid the stigma attached with special needs. It is important to realize that **students with disabilities don't want to be treated any differently**; they just want to participate like anyone else.

Class Size

Depending on the severity of a diagnosed learning disability, some students may require one-on-one instruction while other students with learning disabilities may be able to function in a large class without any accommodation. **Individual assessments and the students' development of coping mechanisms will be the greatest determining factors for how much attention is required by their instructor.** However, don't forget that for most sailors an integral part of the sport is socializing. It will be **important for all students to have a social aspect to their lessons**. Tutorial lessons alone could further stigmatize a student who has problems with self-confidence.

Teaching Style

Students will function better in kinesthetic class situations compared to auditory or visual situations largely because of the level of stimulation provided. Teaching a student with learning disabilities without primarily using kinesthetics will come up short. **Repetition and review, while introducing new topics, will help students with learning disabilities develop confidence.** Reinforcing a student's knowledge base and areas of security will help students with learning disabilities to progress. Focusing on core content areas until mastery and automation will also allow students with learning disabilities to confidently progress.

Reinforcement

Students with learning disabilities are often lacking in self assurance. They may question their competency in areas where you know they are qualified. **Such students with learning disabilities not only enjoy praise for their good work, but also need it to build their self-confidence.** The criticism sandwich should probably be modified slightly for students with learning disabilities to provide more positive reinforcement. Be honest with praise and never sarcastic. Sarcasm will be misinterpreted as a personal attack and false praise will be detected; both of which will cause students to lose confidence in themselves and respect for you.

Routine

Developing a pattern or standard method of operation is essential for students with learning disabilities. Consider for a moment what is involved with change. Change requires that a student learns a new set of rules, a new method of operation. For the student with a learning disability a deviation from a routine can be discouraging. New directions that are given just verbally are difficult for students with learning disabilities to process and understand. For any rules or instructions that you provide, make sure to convey information through multiple methods. Write down the instructions, read and discuss the instructions with students, provide time for an actual demonstration of new procedures (if appropriate), have students actually repeat the new instructions and review the rules.

Lesson Plans

Lessons must be created that keep students active and involved. Idle time is an opportunity to become distracted and/or "space out." **Design lessons that focus on achievable goals.** Students with learning disabilities do *not* benefit from lessons in which they fail. Additionally, **review and reaffirm skills you are teaching.** For instance, after a thorough whiteboard description of an on-the-water drill, have students draw the course on a piece of paper, and then walk through a land drill before hitting the water. Each stage of introducing material, from theory, to concept, to spatial/physical comprehension, to practice allows a student to be successful. (See "Teaching New Skills" in Sections 1 and 2).

Testing and Evaluation

Assessing students with learning disabilities for their knowledge and ability through traditional testing methods will not reflect their true capabilities. Identify what you are truly testing - recall ability or comprehension. Providing the time a student needs to complete a test, not a time limit, will infinitely increase their success on exams. However, open book evaluations and demonstrations of ability may be more appropriate assessment methods for students with learning disabilities. Due to difficulties in written expression, you may find that verbal evaluations allow a student with learning disabilities to convey information more freely. **Remember, sailing is supposed to be FUN**!

Discipline

Ramifications and implications often elude students with learning disabilities. **Providing a highly structured but fair set of rules for behavior and conduct will alleviate discipline concerns.** In fact, create the rules with your students and the rules will carry even more emphasis because the students set their own limits. The old stand-by of "firm, but fair" never had a greater role than in dealing with challenging behavior. Students with learning disabilities retain and repeat things literally. Therefore, say what you mean and mean what you say in both discipline and teaching situations.

Conclusion

Instructing students with learning disabilities won't be much different than any other sailing class. Instructors must simply be *more thorough in planning and designing lessons, and patient in their teaching*. In fact, looking at the demographics of any class will illustrate that you have and will be working with students with a variety of abilities and disabilities. Out of 20 students in a class, you can expect that:

> 70% (14 students) could be predominantly **visual** learners
> 25% (5 students) could be predominantly **auditory** learners
> 5% (1 student) could be a predominantly **kinesthetic** learner
> 60% (12 students) could be **visually impaired**
> 30% (6 students) could have a **learning disability**
> 15% (3 students) could have **Dyslexia**
> 5% (1 student) could be **colorblind**

In general, teaching students with disabilities could be the most rewarding challenge encountered by an instructor. There is no greater opportunity to participate in the triumph of the human spirit. **In preparing yourself to teach students with disabilities, you will need to understand your students' disabilities, patiently support their progress, look to create solutions to seemingly impossible situations, and identify with your students**. After all is said and done, the extrinsic and intrinsic rewards you receive will be well worth the efforts you undertake. Prepare yourself to be amazed!

SECTION 4

RISK MANAGEMENT

SEXUAL HARRASSMENT AND CHILD ABUSE

RISK MANAGEMENT

Almost all human activity involves the **risk** of injury, even teaching sailing. In turn, that **risk** involves the possibility of a lawsuit by the person injured against the person(s) and program organization involved in or in charge of the activity. Those kinds of risks need to be managed, i.e., prevented or minimized at all levels.

The Goals of Risk Management

The primary goals of risk management are:

1) **to try to recognize situations** that could result in harm to person or property and properly deal with them,

2) **to try to reduce the number of small accidents** that cause little harm but happen frequently,

3) **to be prepared for the contingency**, should harm actually occur, so that the harm is kept to a minimum, and

4) **to monitor and adjust** as exposures change and develop.

Sailing is a process which inherently involves a certain amount of risk. Risk management is therefore the sailor's discipline for living with the possibility that future events may cause harm. Given the vagaries of wind, weather, and sailors themselves, perhaps the best watchword should be the motto of the U.S. Coast Guard, *Semper Paratis* (Always Prepared). Your students, their families, your employers, and the sport of sailing depend on *your* judgment and prudence.

That is why program directors, instructors, and all in charge of an instructional program should understand the precepts of risk management as they apply to sailing.

Defining Risk

The initial step for a program and its participants is to understand the wide variety of possible harms that could occur.

Operational risks include the possibility of loss or damage to boats, equipment, personal property, physical property, docks and vehicles used to transport boats and sailors. They also include the possibility of theft or dishonesty.

Legal liability risks include two main areas.

Regulatory risks. These are responsibilities mandated by federal, state and local laws and regulations, such as those requiring launch operators to obtain appropriate licenses, those that stipulate ways to control pollution, those that seek to protect manatees, or those that require powerboats to be registered and inspected. They include exposures such as those of employers to employees, under state workers' compensation acts, the Jones Act and the Longshoremens' and Harborworkers' Act. Regulatory risks have remedies for wrongs such as fines, jail or both, and the violations may be either civil or criminal in nature.

Contracts and tort liability. Contractual liabilities can arise when a party to a written or verbal contract (such as a contract to provide sailing instruction) is held to have violated a responsibility under the terms of the contract. Verbal contracts can be actual or implied, which is why written contracts are advisable for both parties, and injuries can be real or imagined.

Tort liability theories include **negligence**, assault, battery, defamation, invasion of privacy and the like. Most often the tort theory in sailing cases is negligence.

Sailing instructors have a "duty of care" for their students. This is essentially doing or not doing something a reasonably careful person would or would not do. The liabilities are different when you are working with minors.

The **four elements of negligence** must all be present for the court to determine negligence.

① You must have a **legal duty to the injured party**.

② You must have **failed to fulfill your duty**.

③ The **injury had to occur to the party to whom you owed the duty**.

④ Your **failure to fulfill your duty has to be the cause of the injury**.

There are four common **defenses for negligence** available to an instructor.

❶ Show that the **all the elements of negligence were not present**.

❷ Show that the direct causes of the injury were an **act of God** *(forces of nature)*.

❸ Show that the injured party is guilty of *contributory negligence,* meaning that he or she caused the injury. *Comparative negligence* is when a proportion of the fault is distributed among several parties.

❹ Prove that the risk was the *inherent risk* in the sport and that the sailor assumed the risk by engaging in sailing.

Risk Management

In risk management we use a process for dealing with the risk which requires us to first identify those risks. Then evaluate the identified risks for the best treatment. Then deal with the identifed risks.

Risk Identification. First we want to perform a **site assessment**. This involves identifying those areas or items that may lead to an injury. This would mean checking and listing all items and areas around the facility, the docks and the boats themselves. On your list, include even the trivial. The more comprehensive the list the better prepared you will be. Something as simple as a splinter (from a dock covered in creosote) can lead to serious infection and possible gangrene if left unchecked.

Risk Evaluation. Once your comprehensive list is made you can then organize it into one or two categories. One is comprised of areas or items that could lead to frequent and minor injuries; the other could lead to rare and serious injuries. Your goal will be to eliminate or reduce both the seriousness and the frequency of a potential injury.

Risk Resolution. There are four techniques that risk management uses to deal with the identified risks.

1) **Eliminate the risk.** An example would be to correct a problem by fixing a broken dock or not engaging in a particular activity.

2) **Reduce the probabilty that the exposure will lead to serious injury.** An example would be to require sailors to wear shoes.

3) **Assume the risk.** Since students have to go out on the water to sail, an example would be to accept the risk and manage the exposure.

4) **Transfer the risk to a third party.** An example would be to buy lunch from a vendor instead of making lunch for the class or to obtain insurance and have an insurance company take the risk.

Risk Control

Starting with the top priority risks, program organizers should develop a series of responses to try to prevent an occurrence and to be prepared should a contingency happen. They should have a written Emergency Action Plan, and they should have all instructors participate in an actual "practice drill." If some portions of a program are deemed too hazardous, they should be properly removed. For example, an overhead electrical wire anywhere near a small boat launching area is clearly unacceptable. It should be removed or run underground. Other risks can be managed by safety instruction. For example, wearing PFDs at all times on the water may not prevent a drowning but will surely reduce significantly the possibility of one. Still others will require well thought-out emergency planning, such as responses for squalls and similar sudden weather changes.

American Red Cross Emergency Action Plan (EAP) Recommendations

Developing an Emergency Action Plan
An EAP should be developed for any emergency that could occur in a small craft activity. An EAP includes these general features:
- How the person who recognizes the emergency is to signal others
- The steps each person in the group should take in an emergency
- The location of rescue and safety equipment
- Actions to minimize the emergency and safely rescue any victims
- How to call for medical assistance when needed
- Follow-up procedures after an emergency

Before writing your EAP, talk with fellow staff members, volunteer leaders, and participants. If you belong to an agency or organization, check its safety guidelines or consult with the safety officer.

Most emergency action plans include steps for managing specific types of emergencies. For example, an incident involving multiple victims may require coordinating the efforts of different group members.

Contents of an Emergency Action Plan
An emergency action plan should include the following content areas as appropriate:
- ➢ Layout of facility/environment
  - ***Emergency Medical Services (EMS)*** access and entry/exit routes
  - Location of rescue and first aid equipment
  - Location of telephones, with emergency telephone numbers posted
  - Exits and evacuation routes
- ➢ Equipment available
  - Rescue equipment
  - First aid supplies
  - Emergency equipment
- ➢ Support personnel
  - Internal
    - + Staff members
    - + Volunteer leaders
    - + Participants
  - External
    - + **EMS** personnel (police officers and fire fighters)
    - + Search and rescue team and local Coast Guard
    - + Hospitals
- ➢ Staff Responsibilities
  - Assign each person or staff member a duty --
    - + Provide care.
    - + Warn other craft of emergency.
    - + Meet **EMS** personnel.
    - + Interview witnesses.

- ➢ Communication
  - Means available to obtain medical help or access to call 9-1-1
  - The local emergency number, and who will make the call
  - Chain of command
  - Person to contact family/guardian
  - Person to deal with media
- ➢ Follow-up
  - This includes such items as EAP evaluation and documentation. See the following section, "After an Emergency," for a detailed description of follow-up items.

After An Emergency

When an emergency is over, you may need to complete follow-up procedures. For example, you may be responsible for --

- Confirming that witnesses have been interviewed and their observations documented.
- Reporting the incident to the appropriate individual (this may be your supervisor) or authorities.
- Contacting a victim's family/guardian.
- Dealing with the media.
- Inspecting equipment and supplies used in the emergency. Make sure all equipment used is back in place and in good working condition. Replace any used supplies.
- Filling out any report forms and transmitting the reports appropriately.
- Conducting a debriefing or arranging a critical incident stress debriefing. (See next page.)
- Assessing what happened and evaluating the actions taken. You should --
  - -- Review the event as a group.
  - -- Consider what worked well and what could have worked better.
  - -- Change the EAP to correct any weak areas.
  - -- Practice the new plan as soon as possible.

Reports

All injuries and incidents should be documented and reported appropriately. These reports may be used for insurance purposes and in a court of law. Some agencies or organizations may already have a form for this purpose. If not, one can be developed from the sample forms found at the end of this section.

Critical Incident Stress

An emergency involving a serious injury or death is a critical incident. The acute stress it causes an individual can overcome his or her ability to cope. This acute stress is called *critical incident stress.*

Some effects of critical incident stress may appear right away and others may appear after days, weeks, or even months have passed. People suffering from critical incident stress may not be able to perform their jobs well. If not managed properly, this acute stress may lead to a serious condition called post-traumatic stress disorder.

Signs of critical incident stress include the following:

> Confusion
> Lowered attention span; restlessness
> Denial
> Guilt or depression
> Anger
> Anxiety
> Changes in interaction with others
> Increased or decreased eating (weight gain or weight loss)
> Uncharacteristic, excessive humor or silence
> Unusual behavior
> Sleeplessness
> Nightmares

Critical incident stress requires professional help to prevent post-traumatic stress disorder. An individual can reduce stress by --

- Practicing relaxation techniques.
- Eating a balanced diet.
- Avoiding caffeine, alcohol, and drugs.
- Getting enough rest.
- Participating in some type of physical exercise or activity.

Critical Incident Stress Debriefing

A process called critical incident stress debriefing (CISD) brings together a group of people experiencing critical incident stress with some of their peers, such as other staff members, and a trained mental health professional. This process helps those with critical incident stress share and understand their feelings while learning to cope.

Emergency service agencies usually have CISD teams trained to respond and give critical incident stress debriefings. Emergency action plans should include information on obtaining help for managing critical incident stress.

For more information on CISD and stress management, contact: Critical Incident Stress Foundation, 10176 Baltimore National Pike, Suite 201, Ellicott City, Maryland 21042-3652, (410) 750 - 9600, or a local mental health professional.

Reprinted with permission of the American Red Cross from their book Small Craft Safety.

Risk Financing

Funds must be budgeted for a wide variety of risk controls and, in addition, for the more remote possibility that additional costs may be incurred because of loss or damage to property, injury to others, including damage to their property, and regulatory fines. Any program will be wise to have a defined contingency reserve to draw against for smaller cost situations, plus prudent insurance to protect the sponsoring organization, its employees, and volunteers. *Instructors have a right to know exactly what financial protection has been arranged on their behalf by the sponsoring organization.*

The Steps of Risk Management for a Sailing Instructor

As a sailing instructor, there are a number of precautions that you, along with those who arrange and supervise a sailing program, can take to try to ensure a safe program.

1. *Plan your program thoroughly.*
2. *Assess risks on a continuing basis.*
3. *Understand the capabilities and limitations of your students.*
4. *Provide and maintain a safe physical environment.*
5. *Provide and maintain proper equipment.*
6. *Teach state-of-the-art methods.*
7. *Supervise all activities carefull.y*
8. *Prepare and test emergency procedures.*
9. *Maintain complete records of activities.*
10. *Provide appropriate financing for risk.*

Using this approach will give you a good foundation for satisfying many of your legal duties. Let's look at each of these in some detail.

1: Plan your program thoroughly.

Using materials from US SAILING, from prior programs of your sponsoring organization, and from your own experience, develop a complete program of instruction. **Individual lesson plans for each week, and even each day, will be important to the overall continuity of instruction, incorporating the preferable sequence of teaching specific skills, from basic to advanced.**

The program should also **make provision for individual evaluation of each student**. Rate them frequently, discuss their progress, and be prepared to modify your instruction plan to adapt to their progress. **Progress should be recorded in a WRITTEN DOCUMENT** available to students, families, and your sponsoring organization.

2: Assess risks on a continuing basis.

Go back to basic risk evaluation, and review and discuss each type of possible risk with your sponsoring organization and staff *before* your program starts. **RECORD each risk and the suggested response to it,** making sure that each response is prudent, practical and affordable. **Then set responsibilities for assuring that these risks are continually reassessed, in light of new conditions, and that your students and their parents are aware of the risk control standards that have been adopted.**

A <u>Participation Agreement</u> **signed by each student (or a parent/guardian if appropriate)** should be on file before classes begin. In these documents **prospective sailing students acknowledge they they understand the *inherent dangers* involved with sailing** (like capsizing, drowning, head injuries, crushed fingers, etc.) and **yet are willing to assume these risks by indicating that they want to participate in a sailing class.** Signs, orientation meetings and films are also ways to inform prospective sailors about the *inherent dangers* of sailing. The constant repetition of rules and cautions may be annoying, but it will, in the long run, create the appreciation of risk and prudence that will prevent accidents.

SAMPLE NOTIFICATION WARNING STUDENTS ABOUT POLLUTED WATERS...
"The sailing lessons will be given in the waters off (name of sailing center). These waters have been stated to be polluted. All of our instructors have been trained in these waters and in that regard immersed in them on numerous occasions without ill effect. However, there is a risk for any person who comes in contact with these waters and that risk should be clearly known and understood by all participants, parents and/or guardians. In our sailing program or any other similar program, it is inevitable that students come in contact with the water and thereby are exposed to its risks. Any student who falls into the waters will be rinsed with clean water as soon as practicable thereafter -- the optimum that can be done in these circumstances."

3: Understand the capabilities and limitations of your students.

Swimming is the first and most important capability for any student. There is no substitute for a **swimming test**. Next, the program should **assure the physical fitness** of each student for the sailing regimen, including a **complete written health statement** from a responsible person, with any limitations or special medical conditions noted that could affect participation. If in doubt, ask questions. If a student returns to the program after an injury or illness, a physician's statement may be required. Finally, you should **understand the prior sailing experience of each student so that he or she may be placed in the appropriate level of instruction.**

4: Provide and maintain a safe physical environment.

First check the land-based location from which you will be operating. Are the grounds, buildings, and docks safe for your students and their activities? **Under the law you are responsible for both *actual* and *constructive* knowledge of an unsafe condition.** Anything you should have discovered in a regular inspection will be deemed constructive knowledge for which you are still liable. *Actual notice* occurs when the responsible party is given notice of an unsafe condition. To perform your duty, you must provide notice, both *actual notice* and *constructive notice*.

Waivers and "Release of Liability" forms have been very popular for the last several years. Although not always successful at avoiding liability, they have been very effective in providing both actual and constructive notice. Because these types of **forms need to be <u>customized to conform with each state's laws and regulations</u>,** we recommend that each facility/organization's attorney draft a release form that provides actual and constructive notice for their situations. **Make sure that a parent or guardian signs these forms, if you are teaching underage children.**

Then review the waters in which you will be sailing. Are they safe to swim in? Can pollution conditions change? Are floats and moorings safe and inspected periodically?

Facility Inspection Guidelines are an essential component of any safe sailing program and will help to prevent accidents. Conduct inspections each day and each week and keep a record of findings, actions taken to reduce risks and

warnings given about inherent risks. Nearby electrical wires, planking with splinters, sharp edges, exposed nails and similar hazards should be noted and immediate corrections made. If there is a chance of periodic water pollution, learn how to take daily tests -- don't depend on public authorities to warn you.

Finally, since weather conditions can and will change quickly, listen to radio weather forecasts and be prepared to respond to new conditions. If a squall threatens, you should take your students off the water immediately.

5: Provide and maintain proper equipment.

Your program depends on the continued availability of various equipment, owned by you, your sponsoring organization, and/or your students. This equipment should be appropriate, safeguarded, and maintained during the program.

- ☑ **Safety boats and launches** should have proper U.S. Coast Guard and local licenses, as should their operators.
- ☑ **All boats and equipment**, whether owned by the program or by students, **should be inspected daily and the results recorded on a Facility Inspection Form.** If a boat is unsafe or lacks the proper equipment, you should not permit it to be used until the deficiencies are corrected.
- ☑ **Correct operation of a hoist should be taught** (if one is used) and its operation restricted to only those properly instructed in its use. A hoist should be **inspected daily.** Proper written and oral instruction concerning the use of any other equipment or procedures that sailors will use is also important.
- ☑ **Students should be taught responsibility** for their own equipment and respect for the property of others. You can help by providing secure storage areas for all boats, boat parts and personal property. A rash of petty thefts that pit students (and parents) against each other and the instructors can be very debilitating to a program.
- ☑ Many youth programs depend on volunteer parents or others to help transport students, and possibly boats and trailers, to distant regattas. Be sure that all **volunteer drivers so involved are properly licensed and insured and that their towing equipment is appropriate.**

6: **Teach state-of-the-art methods.**

Your instruction program should embody state-of-the-art teaching methods, incorporating US SAILING guidelines and your experience plus that of other instructional staff and the sponsoring organization. The sailing program should provide skill-level appropriate instruction as well as feedback. You should **utilize resources such as *Start Sailing Right!* that support US SAILING guidelines and are recognized as the "standard of excellence" in the sport of sailing.**

Follow carefully the instruction plan you have drawn up, and make substitutions only with the approval of the sponsoring organization. Keep up with new sailing and teaching advances by reading current sailing publications, attending relevant symposiums and conferences and using newly-developed audio-visual tools that become available.

Proper instruction also presupposes careful selection of instructional staff and assurance that each staff member has been qualified. **Do all instructors have first aid and CPR training? Are they certified by US SAILING? Do they have the necessary required valid U.S. Coast Guard, state and automobile licenses**?

7: **Supervise activities carefully.**

Supervision is a major responsibility, especially when younger students are involved. It begins before your students arrive at the sailing site and continues until after the last student has left for the day. At times it will require *General Supervision* and at other times it may require *Specific Supervision*. This supervision will include not only the students but also your staff. A Program Director or Head Instructor has the overall responsibility even when he or she is not out on the water with a particular sailing class or near the activity in which they are engaged.

General supervision requires you to be in the area of the activity at all times to not only keep the program going but also to try to anticipate problems. *Specific supervision* of the sailors will be required at times when there is a higher risk of an injury. This might involve activities such as teaching a new sailing skill, conducting a swim test or responding to an emergency.

Supervision means maintaining a level of discipline appropriate to the activity. Hazing, raucous behavior and horseplay on or near the water can all lead to accidents and injury if not controlled. You certainly do not have to be a drill sergeant, but you must remain in control of activities. If a student is reprimanded or punished for inappropriate behavior, record the circumstances and discuss the situation with your sponsoring organization (and both parents if the student is a minor). Disruptive behavior can destroy both the fun and the learning process for other students, so prompt and effective action can be essential to the success of your program.

Consider also the recommended instructor-to-student and safety-boat-to-students-on-the-water ratios when deciding on levels of supervision. One of the most frequent complaints in sports lawsuits involves the allegation of "failure to supervise." *The degree of supervision must be related to the degrees of potential risk.*

8: Prepare and test emergency procedures.

Emergencies can and will occur. You should **have <u>written procedures</u> for a wide range of possible events, and you and your staff should TEST your ability to respond** quickly and appropriately. (See the American Red Cross Emergency Action Plan (EAP) Recommendations earlier in this chapter, the Emergency Response Recommendations on the next page and the sample Emergency Form at the end of this section.) **Are you ready to handle:**

☑ a capsized boat?

☑ an overboard recovery?

☑ a serious injury to a student (both at the dock and on the water)?

☑ a safety boat breakdown?

☑ the theft of critical equipment?

☑ a sudden change in weather conditions?

The real practice of risk management begins when you are forced to respond to an emergency, especially one in which several things go wrong at the same time.

☑ Do you have the required first aid and CPR skills?

☑ Can you communicate immediately from either land or water with professional emergency teams?

☑ Do you know the emergency number for your area? (Not all areas have 911 systems in place.)

☑ Do you know the location of, way to and distance to the nearest hospital emergency facilities?

The emergency plans that you prepare for a variety of risk scenarios should be reviewed carefully with your staff, your sponsoring organization and your local response team. These plans should be specific to your site and updated as appropriate.

---

① EMERGENCY RESPONSE RECOMMENDATIONS...

IN AN EMERGENCY:
1. *Call 911* (if applicable).
2. *Call the appropriate agency(ies), i.e.* Search & Rescue 555-714, Non-emergency Police   555-766, or Non-emergency Sheriff 555-742.

YOU SAY:
☑ "This is an emergency. The telephone I am calling from is 123-4567."
☑ Exact nature of accident.
☑ Medical assessment of victim.
☑ Exact location of accident.
☑ Description of victim and victim's name.
☑ Your name.
☑ Provide driving directions for emergency vehicle to get **to where the emergency is** -- which may or may not be the facility's address.
Do not hang up until the operator has hung up.

9: Maintain complete records of activities.

Each day an instructor should complete a *Log* (written record) of all sailing program activities, noting:

☑ weather and water conditions periodically, as well as significant changes

☑ names of absent students

☑ incidents involving possible injury, physical damage or loss

☑ conditions calling for repairs

☑ any other events of note

Each day the senior instructor should review and approve the Log, and each week's Logs should be reviewed by an appropriate supervisory authority. The Logs should be maintained as a permanent record. Should litigation occur, the Logs may be indispensable for defense.

Similarly, you should maintain in the records your **Emergency Action Plan and any accident reports** given to medical, police or insurance organizations. **These records should also include any participation agreements, waivers, releases, or hold harmless agreements** signed by students (or parents/guardians when applicable), **student medical forms, progress reports on students, periodic facility inspection reports, and your daily/weekly lesson plans**. (See sample forms at end of this section.)

10: Provide appropriate financing for risk.

Those sponsoring a sailing program should assure themselves, and their instructional staff, that **adequate funds are available to meet the possible contingencies** described in the risk assessment. This may mean the use of a special reserve fund or budget to cover the smaller losses that inevitably occur in any program. This also means provision of appropriate forms of insurance to protect the sponsoring organization, its employees, its members (if a club), its volunteers, and its instructional staff (if not employees). They should be protected from a variety of risks, including, but not limited to, physical damage to property, dishonesty and theft, legal liability, automobile liability, marine liability, workers' compensation, and the possibility of fines (if insurable). The details of this financing should be explained in full to the instructional staff so that they will understand their rights, duties and responsibilities, especially for insurance.

For example, if a sponsoring organization carries a deductible on its liability insurance policy that covers instructors, will that organization reimburse an instructor if he or she is sued and the deductible is imposed? Has the sponsoring organization provided proper workers' compensation protection, including Jones Act and comparable coverage? Has its automobile liability insurance been extended to cover non-owned vehicles, such as those used by instructors and volunteers? All of these areas of risk financing should be confirmed before starting a program. If your program supervisor does not include this imformation during staff training, ask!

The sponsoring organization can seek assistance from US SAILING and other specialists in determining what insurance may be appropriate and what limits of protection are prudent. Special insurance coverages are also available from programs endorsed by US SAILING for events such as regattas and through US SAILING for certified instructors. Specific details can be obtained from US SAILING.

Documentation and Record Keeping

We can't over emphasize the importance of <u>proper documentation</u>. <u>Maintain a complete record of all forms, agreements, reports, checklists, etc.</u> If an injury occurs and a lawsuit results, complete documentation of your efforts will be essential. **You must maintain records of all actions taken to avoid an accident and what actually happened.** These records may be all you have to show a jury that you acted in a prudent and professional manner, and may very well be the difference in prevailing in a lawsuit.

Examples of Risk Management Situations

Each of the following cases involves risk, the chance that some future event may cause injury or harm to person or property. Each may also affect the success of your teaching program and the confidence that your sponsoring organization, students and their families have in your ability. Beyond that, a failure in judgment could mean a lawsuit and a black mark against the sport of sailing. If you have carefully followed the steps and responsibilities of risk management as outlined by this section, you will be able to answer the questions.

1) **You are in your second year of teaching in Boston. Several of your returning sailors from last year's class want some early practice on a Saturday in late May. It's hot -- an uncharacteristic 90 degrees -- but you know the water temperature is still in the fifties. How do you advise these sailors?**

   You advise your students about the risks of hypothermia in the cold early spring waters off Boston and the importance of dressing appropriately, and you mandate that the sailors wear PFDs and sail only when accompanied by a safety boat.

2) **Boats are being readied for sailing off Washington's Bainbridge Island. It's slow at the hoist so one crew, with their boat fully rigged, decides to push their trailer to the other end of the grounds to launch at a ramp. What is your immediate concern?**

Before allowing a crew to move their rigged boat to the launching ramp, you will check for overhead wires, determine whether the ramp is clean and free of debris, and provide proper supervision.

3) **You're in the fourth week session at a summer camp in Louisiana. The heat is stifling and the humidity on the lake leaves you dripping with sweat. Ten doublehanded dinghies are setting out for a two-hour class. How should these sailors be prepared for the weather conditions?**

Facing a day of high heat and humidity, your students should be wearing sun-protective gear and carrying plenty of liquids.

4) **One of your students tells you she is missing $20 from the ditty bag she left on shore during class. How do you respond?**

After an alleged theft, you will make a prompt investigation, report to students, parents (when applicable) and supervisors, and provide a secure place to store valuables in the future.

5) **It's a typical hot, humid, and almost windless day on the Chesapeake Bay. Your sailors have almost completed their schedule of races, with only one short windward/leeward race remaining before calling it a day. Over on the western shore, however, a rising green-brown cloud mass foretells an afternoon squall, in which winds can reach 60 knots. Do you send your boats to the beach or try to get in the last race?**

With a vicious squall imminent, you will send your students ashore to safety, well before the squall hits. Remember the motto, "When in doubt, don't go out!"

Risk Management Conclusion

Risk management in sailing is essentially common sense. Cautious seamen respect the sea, its power and vagaries, and the fragility of their equipment. This essential caution will be taught by prudent sailing instructors to their students, using the tools of risk assessment, risk control, and risk financing, to assure a safe and secure program -- one that enhances the joy of the sport of sailing.

Even with all of these precautions taken, an accident can still happen. It may also end up in court with a judge awarding damages to the injured party, even though you feel you performed as well as anyone could have in the same situation. Our ultimate goal is for you, as an instructor, to be confident in knowing that you have done everything that could have been done in each situation to ensure a safe program for all.

SEXUAL HARASSMENT AND CHILD ABUSE

In today's world everyone must be aware of certain sensitivities whether they be to gender, ethnic origin, disability, age, sexual preference, etc. Instructors must be aware of all these concerns whether they are dealing with adults or children. They must be aware of, or become aware of, what is considered an appropriate interaction with a student.

It is imperative that instructors learn how to safely and responsibly interact with their students since our society is filled with an increasing awareness of personal boundaries and personal rights as they relate to discrimination, sexual harassment, and abuse. Instructors are often idolized, and so they need to be careful about their interactions with students.

Instructors must learn how to protect themselves against misinterpretations or allegations of abuse or harassment. Finally, instructors must become aware of their responsibility to take action if they suspect that a student may be a victim of abuse or if a student tells an instructor about being abused.

As an instructor, you are vulnerable to charges of sexual harassment or physical abuse. Here are some precautions to help deter accusations.

Appropriate Touch

- **Avoid situations where you are isolated and one on one with a student.** Always be in view of others. If someone misinterprets your actions, it is his or her word against yours.

- **Don't initiate physical contact.** But if, for example, a child initiates a hug, then it is appropriate to respond in kind.

- **Play it safe.** What you may consider a helpful act, such as putting sunscreen on a student's back, may make that adult or child feel uncomfortable or sexually violated. An innocent gesture can be misinterpreted!

- **Use good judgment.** Be aware of personal space and interactions and act upon any suspected or known physical or sexual abuse.

Physical Abuse

The statistics on physical abuse are alarming. Of the estimated hundreds of thousands of abuse victims battered each year, thousands die. For those who survive, the emotional trauma remains long after the external bruises have healed. Communities and courts have recognized that these emotional "hidden bruises" can be treated. Students who have been abused may display:

- ☑ Poor self-image
- ☑ Inability to rely on or trust others
- ☑ Aggressive and disruptive behavior
- ☑ Passive or withdrawn behavior
- ☑ School or job failures
- ☑ Alcohol or drug abuse

Battering is not the only kind of abuse. Many students are victims of neglect, sexual abuse, and emotional abuse.

Sexual Abuse and Children

If a child tells an adult that he or she has been sexually abused, the adult may feel uncomfortable and not know what to say or do. At a minimum, offer the child protection and take action to stop the abuse. Although laws vary from one state to another, the proper authorities, such as the local Protection Agency, the Police or the District Attorney's office must be notified of any concerns of abuse.

SECTION 5

THE CORINTHIAN SPIRIT

THE CORINTHIAN SPIRIT

KEY CONCEPTS TO TEACH
- Sailing as a Corinthian Sport
- Rules Compliance
- Student/Crew First
- Good Behavior
- Sportsmanship

Corinthian Behavior Expected of an "Experienced" Sailor

Sailors are on their own once they are finished with their instruction. They must consolidate all their previous learning materials and sailing skills and move into the world of sailing. Their behavior with other sailors and future guests/crew should follow the accepted code of ethics known as the Corinthian Spirit. This theme is what experienced sailors strive constantly to attain so they can keep things in proper perspective.

Corinthian sailing traditions, passed down through the years, have formed the foundation of the sport. You, as an instructor, need to help beginners understand what this Corinthian Spirit is. Unlike soccer where there is an official in a black and white striped jersey, sailing is a self-policing activity. In the Racing Rules of Sailing it says:

> *"Competitors in the sport of sailing are governed by a body of rules that they are expected to follow and enforce. A fundamental principle of sportsmanship is that when competitors break a rule they will promptly take a penalty or retire."*

All the rules of sailing and the accepted behavior code rely on skippers and crew acting above reproach and "policing" themselves which requires the highest standards of sportsmanship. They must help each other out in emergencies at sea. This is all part of the Corinthian Spirit.

History and Hollywood have painted a rather bleak view of the sailor. Such catch phrases as "cusses like a sailor" and characters like "Captain Bligh" and "Blackbeard" give a non-sailor the impression that sailors are an undisciplined lot. Recent events like the 1995 America's Cup in San Diego have not always shown sailing in its most corinthian light. Sometimes, even local sailboat races don't look like fun since there is too much yelling.

Many long-time sailors will insist that this is not a true picture of sailing today. However, if you go to almost any race course in the country, the prevailing attitude is "winning is everything." Because there is only going to be one winner, there are usually more unhappy sailors. Some will say the race committee did not do something right; others might say there was a problem with the handicap system. The bottom line for the new sailor is that "serious" sailing in races or in heavy air does not look like much fun due to all the high emotion, yelling and clashing egos.

Teaching the Corinthian Spirit. You have instructed your students on correct sailing techniques. You have covered theories of how a boat sails. You have provided information on how to sail safely. Now it is time to give your students a foundation upon which to build their new sailing life - teach them about the Corinthian Spirit.

Gary Jobson, well-known sailor and TV commentator, summed up what sailing means to him this way: "I have sailed all types of boats, all around the world and what makes sailing so rewarding are the people and friends you sail with." This is an extremely important point, and it is imperative that you provide sailors with all the necessary skills so they can achieve this outcome. There are many reasons people sail - to be with friends, to be outdoors, for relaxation, for adventure, to race, etc. All of these are Corinthian activities, and all should be pursued in a Corinthian manner. Proper behavior is part of this, and so you, the instructor, are a role model for your new students. After your students finish their sailing lessons with you, they will emulate your code of conduct whenever they are the skipper or crew on other boats.

Proper Behavior. The Corinthian Spirit is often referred to as good sportsmanship, but it also includes relating to other people with integrity, respect, patience, good judgment, courtesy and unselfishness. Living up to these standards is a challenge which must be taught and practiced like any other skill. Sailors need to work on staying in emotional control even at stressful times, or sailing will not be enjoyed by all. One way to try to do this is to encourage a sailor to have his/her priorities in proper perspective. Is getting somewhere fast what is important or is it important to get there safely and have fun while doing so?

Student/Crew First

The Corinthian Spirit will work its way into your instructional program since your students' goals and desires should be the focus of your instruction. In business the customer comes first, and all business activity revolves around supplying the customer with what they want when they want it. This basic concept of "supply and demand" applies to new sailors.

Goals and Desires (Demands) of New Sailors

An equal opportunity to participate
A safe learning environment
Dynamic and qualified instructors
An enjoyable and successful learning experience
Training to the level of one's abilities
Respectful treatment
Special attention, if needed

If you structure your sailing program to meet these goals (demands), you will not only provide a wonderful learning opportunity but also provide what your students want and need. With today's "winning is everything" attitude, sometimes the proper focus is lost. When this focus is lost, teachers and instructors start to measure success based on ***their*** goals, rather than their students' goals. A good coach will tell you that the most important person on a 50 member team is the 50th person. This good coach or teacher will not spend more time with the top athletes/students but will treat everyone equally. If a coach or teacher (as well as the other students) do not focus on the 50th person, then next week there will only be 49 people, and so on and so on...

Crew First. When a sailor becomes a skipper, he/she needs to remember that each other sailor and/or crew member will have goals and desires ("demands"). Skippers have to not only try to help crew members meet these goals but also accept responsibility for the lives and safety of their crew.

Goals and Desires (Demands) of Crew

Proper training and practice for the tasks expected
Patience and understanding from the skipper
Proper safety equipment on the boat
Proper gear and clothing for the conditions expected
An opportunity to learn all positions on a boat
An understanding that any mistakes/accidents are the responsibility of the skipper

Proper Priorities. What most people desire is the love, respect and admiration of their family, friends and peers. Sailors need to keep this priority in mind when they are in stressful situations on-the-water.

Emotional Control - Handling the "Disaster"

Instructors try not to put students into situations which they are not yet capable of handling, and skippers try not to put themselves and their crew in such stressful situations. But such "disasters" do happen and sometimes there are charged emotional responses like "yelling."

If you analyze behaviors such as too much "yelling," the cause of the stress is usually a lack of control (both real and emotional). When skippers lose control of their boats and/or themselves, they are scared not only because they are concerned about the safety of their boat but also because they feel a responsibility for the crew who are often family and friends. When confronted with a "disaster" beyond one's control, many undesirable behaviors tend to come out. Inexperience is the bottom line from which most of these behaviors stem.

Good quality sailing instruction should recognize that stressful situations are going to arise and should offer a chance to practice during the learning process the appropriate emotional response when a "disaster" strikes. Responding correctly to these anticipated moments with behavior that is consistent with the Corinthian Spirit helps everyone gain confidence in and respect for each other. This awareness also means that unwanted behaviors can be worked on by both skippers and crew. Instructors should encourage the "Corinthian Spirit" as a way to stay in balance with the constant challenges that sailing offers. As an instructor, a practical way of instilling this theme is through the concept of sportsmanship.

Sportsmanship

Good sportsmanship is critical to sailing if it is going to be a rewarding experience for sailors. Good sportsmanship means proper behavior, and, in sailing, involves rules compliance and protests, when necessary. Without it many sailors become frustrated and lose the respect of fellow sailors. Good sportsmanship is an important standard of behavior that is not only pertinent to sailing but also to life. As 4-time Olympic Gold Medalist Paul Elvstrom wrote:

> *"You haven't won the game if in winning the game you have lost the respect of your competitors."*

Examples of Sportsmanlike Behavior

Follow the rules of sailing as they are meant to be played.
If you break a rule, promptly take a penalty or retire.
Protest any non-compliance with the rules.
Tell a sailor or a team of sailors that they have done something well.
Thank the race committee members, judges, umpires and regatta organizers.
Always try your best whether you are first or last.
Behave properly so the sailing is fun for everyone.
Be tolerant and supportive of others who are trying their hardest but who make
    mistakes or cannot do something as well as you.
Share tips and information that can help others so that the sailing is more
    challenging and fun for everyone.

Examples of Unsportsmanlike Behavior

Cheating and trying to get away with rules infractions.
Not lodging a protest when someone has clearly gained an advantage from a rules
    violation.
Yelling at a teammate, competitor or official in an angry tone of voice.
Complaining about the fairness of the teams or a "call" by an official.
Making excuses when things don't go your way.
Arguing about who won or lost.

Making others feel badly after you've won.

Making the winners feel badly when you haven't won.

Swearing.

Stealing from other competitors.

Physical meanness to others, no matter who started it.

Acting in a way that wastes the time of others so that it is harder to get something done.

Behaving in any manner that causes others to lose respect for you.

Football Coach Vince Lombardi is credited with the saying "winning is everything." What he actually said was "the desire to win is everything." Instructors should not let the "desires" of future sailors cloud their judgment.

Competitor Moral Ponderings

Situation #1

A. You are approaching the jibe mark just a few feet clear astern of another boat and decide that it is crucial to get an overlap. You reach back, lower your auxiliary engine, fire it up and propel yourself into an overlap.

B. You are approaching the jibe mark just a few feet clear astern of another boat and decide that it is critical to get an overlap. You rock your boat several times propelling yourself into an overlap.

Could you ever imagine yourself in scenario A? Could you every imagine yourself in scenario B? If you did this on the water (in the heat of the moment), could you imagine yourself admitting to it on shore and dropping out of the race? Is there any difference between the actions in the two scenarios? Are the actions in either scenario ever justifiable?

Situation #2

You are crewing at a district championship that qualifies the top finishing boat for the class world championship. After measurement and before the first race, the owner of the boat asks you to help him remove the lead weight that the boat is required to carry. He justifies the action on the basis that all the other top guys are doing it, so it's OK.

Would you ever consider doing this? Are there any circumstances where this is justifiable? What are some of your options at this point? What would you do?

Situation #3

A. You are lining up to start with about one minute left to go, and you notice that the boat just to leeward has a huge hunk of seaweed wrapped on its rudder.

B. You are on the first windward leg of a race and notice that the boat to leeward of you is about to run over a slightly submerged log that they apparently don't see.

Would you notify the sailors in either scenario of the situations they were facing? If you didn't, would this still be considered good sportsmanship?

Situation #4

You are sailing in an open class under a handicap system. Your boat is rated fast, and you owe the other boats a lot of time. After sailing for five hours in very light air, you are nearing the finish with a nice lead. Then you notice that the breeze is filling in from behind and bringing up all your competitors. Because of the new breeze all the boats finish right behind you, and you lose on corrected time. After the race you overhear your competitors congratulating each other on their great race.

What would you do in this situation?

Instructor Moral Ponderings

Situation #1

You have a beginning class you are teaching with several other instructors helping out. One of the instructors is a 19 year old, and on extremely hot days he takes off his shirt and teaches with no shirt on?

Is this appropriate? Would the situation be the same if the instructor was female?

Situation #2

You have a student who is chronically late. You talk to the student and upon further examination you find out that his/her mother is the driver and her work schedule dictates a different starting time than yours.

What sort of action can you take? What would you do if this scenario applied to one of your instructors?

Situation #3

One of your instructors is disciplining an aggressive 16 year old sailor. After the confrontation the young sailor walks away and you hear, "F____ you."

As the Head Instructor, what sort of action should you take?

Situation #4

You have a 19 year old instructor who appears to be flirting with a 17 year old student in the class.

How would you handle the situation?

Situation #5

On the second day of class a 42 year old student comes and tells you she doesn't want to sail with Jack because he is not learning quickly enough. She wants to sail with Phil because he already has a good grasp of how to sail?

How would you handle this?

Situation #6

In the middle of your program Susie and Ann tell you they can't sail with Bill because he won't listen to them. He just keeps saying, "You don't know anything."

How would you handle this?

Situation #7

Of the 20 students in your class, 10 are doing very well, 5 are improving, but the last 5 are not progressing well at all. They are not happy about this, and one of your better sailors says, "Don't worry; they aren't going to be coming anymore anyway."

How would you handle this?

The Corinthian Spirit

Good sportsmanship, rules compliance, helping other sailors, putting your student/crew first, good behavior and prioritizing values all add up to the Corinthian Spirit. This spirit is the theme that will guide not only sailors but also instructors. It provides the framework within which sailors can pursue their own personal goals and have fun with friends.

Sportsmanship Water Drill

To practice sportsmanship, have your class do a good sportsmanship race. In order to "win" the race, a sailor must be judged by his/her peers as the best "sport". This type of game not only becomes great fun but also brings a new perspective to how the proper "Corinthian Spirit" makes this fun possible.